THE COMPLETE DI COOKBOOK AND STORING FOOD GUIDE

How To Dehydrate And Storing Food With Healthy Recipes For Use Your Dried Food

Amaranta Keller

© Copyright 2020 by Amaranta Keller

All rights reserved.

This document is geared towards providing exact and reliable information with regards to the topic and issue covered. The publication is sold with the idea that the publisher is not required to render accounting, officially permitted, or otherwise, qualified services. If advice is necessary, legal or professional, a practiced individual in the profession should be ordered.

- From a Declaration of Principles which was accepted and approved equally by a Committee of the American Bar Association and a Committee of Publishers and Associations.

In no way is it legal to reproduce, duplicate, or transmit any part of this document in either electronic means or in printed format. Recording of this publication is strictly prohibited and any storage of this document is not allowed unless with written permission from the publisher. All rights reserved.

The information provided herein is stated to be truthful and consistent, in that any liability, in terms of inattention or otherwise, by any usage or abuse of any policies, processes, or directions contained within is the solitary and utter responsibility of the recipient reader. Under no circumstances will any legal responsibility or blame be held against the publisher for any reparation, damages, or monetary loss due to the information herein, either directly or indirectly.

Respective authors own all copyrights not held by the publisher.

The information herein is offered for informational purposes solely, and is universal as so. The presentation of the information is without contract or any type of guarantee assurance.

The trademarks that are used are without any consent, and the publication of the trademark is without permission or backing by the trademark owner. All trademarks and brands within this book are for clarifying purposes only and are the owned by the owners themselves, not affiliated with this document.

(Page intentionally left blank)

TABLE OF CONTENTS

Introduction 1
Chapter 1: Dehydrating Your Food 10
Chapter 2: Dehydration And Other Methods Of Food Preservation 24
Chapter 3: Dehydrating Techniques: How To Achieve Best Results 37
Chapter 4: Ideal Dehydrating Temperature For Various Foods And Fruits
.... 43
Chapter 5: Healthy Living And Diet Tips 49
Recipes 64
   How To Dehydrate And Use Vegetables, Meat And…. Much More .. 64
   Dehydrated Tomatoes (Dried Tomatoes) 67
   Broccoli 73
   Cabbage 76
   Carrots 80
   Onions 84
   Onion Flakes 86
   Dehydrate Corn 87
Strawberries 89
Dry Snack 91
   Pumpkin Chips Baking Recipe 91
   Beet Chips 94
   Dried Kale Chips 96
   Beef Jerky 99
   Canadian-Style Ham And Bacon 107
   Grated Fruit And Vegetable Salad 109
Desserts 111
   Lavashak 111
   Very Spicy Gingerbread Cookies 115
   Raw Crackers 117

Chocolate And Banana Fruit Roll	120
Peanut Butter Banana Chips	121
Conclusion	123

INTRODUCTION

From time immemorial, man has keenly involved himself in the activity of storing food. The only assurance of having enough to eat is through reserving the food available for consumption and keeping the food in good conditions. Doing this would ensure that the stored food remains edible, even when it is needed for consumption at a future time.

As human beings attain a higher level of civilization and technological advancement, we equally develop our methods of preserving foods. A good method will not only ensure that the food is well preserved, it will also ensure that the preserved food becomes more nourishing and beneficial to our health.

Through healthy preservative methods, foods are brilliantly sufficient for planned consumption, healthy growth and sweeter tastes.

The traditional cycle of harvesting crops or hunting animals and consuming them, cannot work without an intersecting process of preservation. This is because the harvested crops are usually much more than the specific quantity a famer and his family members can immediately consume. Equally, there is a very narrow chance that the farmer or hunter would sell his entire produce and hunt in a single visit to the market. Even when this happens, the buyers of the farmer's produce would need to reserve the excesses in order to consume at a later time.

Food storage or food preservation is any method by which food is kept from spoilage for, before and after immediate consumption.

Storing food therefore comes from the question; how do we keep the excesses of the moment for beneficial use in the future?

In response to the question posed, human beings have made several inventions. These inventions include various methods of storage and these methods have greatly helped in preserving and enriching our foods.

This guide will bring one of these methods of preservation – Dehydrating, under the microscope, for amplified examination. Before that is achieved, however, we shall examine all the methods of preservations briefly.

The oldest methods of storing our food includes; drying, fermentation and refrigeration. Drying involves the application of any form of dry heat on food in other to avoid spoilage. Fermentation involves converting the state of food or food drink by leaving it for a period of time, in order to allow chemical reactions occur. Refrigeration is the process of applying cold temperature to food in order to keep it healthy for consumption.

More recent methods of preservation are; pasteurization, canning, freezing, irradiation, addition of chemicals and mechanical drying.

It is impossible to talk about dehydration or any of the methods of preservation without critically examining some terms or registers under the topic. First among these is 'Food spoilage'.

What is Food spoilage?

Food spoilage is any reaction that occurs to our food and makes it unhealthy to our health. Any process that renders a nourishing food into an unhealthy food is spoilage. The process may be the product of different factors. It may be due to infestation by microorganisms, degradation by endogenous enzymes which are already members of the food particles while it was still in its healthy state, contamination due to insects or other living organisms or mere careless pollution which may be the unintentional addition of poisonous substances.

Foods may also spoil based on reactions from other spoiled foods. If you mix healthy food with spoiled one, the spoiled one will naturally spoil the healthy food in a short time.

The process of food spoilage starts from the very moment the farmer harvests his crops from the farm, or when the hunter kills his prey.

The enzymes contained in the cells of plant and animal tissues may be released as a result of any mechanical damage inflicted during postharvest handling. These enzymes begin to break down the cellular material.

Evidences of food spoilage involves; changes in coloration of food, changes in taste (usually, spoiled foods tastes sour), deterioration of texture, shrinking (in cases of vegetables and fruits), emitting of odor, etc.

The essence of storing food safely is to keep them healthy as bacteria are fond of infesting improperly stored foods. When a bacterial attacks a food particle, it takes only a few moments on it before it begins to multiply sporadically.

The space between these sporadic increases in number is the time it takes the bacterial to acclimatize itself with the new clime. This is referred to as the lag phase.

The log phase is the following stage where the number of bacteria grows increasingly. As the number of bacteria keeps getting higher, the infesters eat up the healthy nutrients in the food and not only do they leave the unhealthy portions but they also excrete on it. The waste products of these infesters and the depleted supply of nutrient in the food both stop the growing speed of the bacteria. The number or size is then kept static. At this stage, the bacteria can neither have higher growth nor reduce in number. This is called the stationary phase. For every increase in the number of bacteria, there is an immediate decrease. So the number of the bacteria remains constant for the remaining period.

Another food storing term is 'Temperature'. The temperature of a food will influence the storage and longevity. In very cold climes, matters generally maintain their state for a long period of time. This explains the involvement of refrigerating gadgets in storing foods.

Historically, extinct mammals such as mammoths and lemmings

were discovered millions of years after their extinction because they travelled in herds to the Antarctica. Despite their deaths, their bodies were preserved as freshly as they had been at the time of their death because of the cold temperature in their burial zones. Many intact bodies were dug out from huge glaciers. This historical account highlights the essence of temperature on preserving our food.

While the addition of heat makes many food edible by converting from its raw states. Excess heat will adversely affect the state of the food.

Temperature therefore plays a vital role in the storage of food and drinks.

It is important to also briefly talk about the Classes of Food. Commonly, we have seven major classes of food, they are; Proteins, Carbohydrates, Fats and Oil, Minerals, Fibers, Vitamins and Water.

We shall examine these classes briefly;

Proteins: Proteins are nutrients that build our body. They make up the building blocks of our muscles, skins, hormones and organs. They repair and maintain tissues. Milk products, meats, legumes, fish and beans are rich examples of proteins. The molecules of proteins, chiefly includes oxygen, hydrogen, nitrogen and carbon.

The function of foods that contains proteins includes maintaining healthy muscles, building cells and improving metabolism. Amino acids are one of the basic constituents of proteins. Essential proteins are proteins that can be produced in our bodies and a protein that cannot be produced in the body is called Non-essential.

Carbohydrates: Carbohydrates gives the body energy. These contains sugars and starches found in foods; grains, vegetables, fruits and milk. They are often maligned in most foods; they are important part of our meals. Examples are wheat, rice, potatoes, maize and other starchy meals. They are made up of molecules which contains oxygen, carbon and hydrogen atoms.

Carbohydrates are classified according to the amount of monomer units they contain. The monomer units are polysaccharides, monosaccharaides and disaccharides.

Fats and Oil: Fats and Oils provide energy to the body and they regulate the body temperature. They also absorb vitamins. Dairy products; fish, meats, eggs, ground nuts, and vegetables are rich examples of fats and oil. Fruits such as avocado and nuts are rich fruit examples.

Molecules of Fats and oil are made up of chiefly of hydrogen atoms and long chains of carbon. Fats and oil can be grouped into unsaturated and saturated fats.

Unsaturated fats and oils are fats that have carbon connected with double bonds and a few molecules of hydrogen while Saturated fats have all carbon atoms bonded to hydrogen atoms. Subsequently, I shall explain the proper proportions for consuming the groups.

Minerals: Minerals are cellulose collections which are a part of carbohydrate that is not completely absorbed by humans. Minerals are not digested by the body of humans because of the absence of its digestive enzymes but they are essential for digestion. Fruits and vegetables are rich fiber constituents. Whole grains and pulses are further examples.

Although diets that contain fibers usually prevent coronary diseases of the heart, cancers of the bowels and diabetes. The major essence of fiber is to keep our digestive systems healthy. Fiber also stabilizes our glucose and cholesterol levels.

Minerals are responsible for strong and healthy muscles, teeth and bones. Strong bones help us carry oxygen in our bodies and minerals helps to keeps body fluids balanced. All living things need calcium, zinc, irons, potassium, and magnesium etc. which are all examples of minerals. Minerals examples include dairy products, meats, fish, grains and poultry.

Vitamins: Vitamins are consumed in small quantities but they are a very important class of food. Vitamins helps the body develop immunity against harmful materials are they are also important in regulating the immune system. Riboflavin, Folic Acid, Ascorbic acid, Biotin Niacin, Thiamime, Cynacobalamin etc. are major examples of vitamins.

All food products contain vitamins and they are very beneficial to the human body.

Water: Water is the healthy fluid that is taken into the body system. It is essential for easy transportation of useful elements within the body. 80% of our body system is filled with water. It is a simple combination of Hydrogen and Oxygen (H2O). Water is necessary for bodily fluids and the digestive processes. The body acidity is maintained by water at the proper level. Virtually every food and fruits contains a level of water.

In various preservative methods, nutrients are destroyed and many diets have little or no nutritional value to the consumer. This guide will help you see how to engage dehydration accurately in ways that reduces minimal nutrient loss.

Only a few people are aware that when dehydrating, not all dehydration methods are exposed to the same degree of heat. This guide will give the accurate degree of heat needed for the varieties of food we have. This guide will also expose the effect of the heat exposition on food and how lost nutrients can be replenished in certain conditions.

The level of heat applied to a food during dehydration is subject to certain conditions including the class of food, mass and weight of the diet, capability of the food and the specific consumption period etc.

Dehydration – which will be our major concern in this guide, is one of the oldest methods of storing food. Through the years, there have been several developments in how human beings dehydrate their food.

At first, people used simply sun drying method. Sun drying involves spreading the food outside in an open space where it is exposed to the heat generated from the sunlight. In modern times, various dehydrating machines have been built to provide artificial sources of heat in various degrees.

One of the greatest advantages of dehydrating food or applying heat to our food, as indicated earlier, is that it truncates the growth of microorganisms and bacteria. Under heat, it is impossible for bacteria to grow on our foods. Another major edge of dehydrating food is the convenience.

When our foods are properly dehydrated, they can change forms and serve as spices for other food or consumed as individual snacks. The change in texture and taste also makes the dehydrated food nutritious accomplices of other foods.

Dehydrated food can also function as medicines for some certain ailments or as protective materials such as analgesics. They can also be converted into beauty care products or fragrances.

For some food, simply dehydrating them can extend their life span to a very long period. For example, in some cases, consistent dehydration can keep the food for as long as twenty to thirty years.

This guide is sufficient in providing all the information needed to stay guided on dehydrating all classes and kinds of foods. It also provides the best methods of storing our foods. The guide also compares varieties of storing methods with advantages and disadvantages of each method mentioned.

CHAPTER 1
DEHYDRATING YOUR FOOD

Dehydration in relation to food storage can be defined as the process in which foods are preserved, through the removal or reduction of moisture. This reduction can keep the dehydrated food in healthy condition for a long period of time. Microorganisms and bacteria cannot endure reduction of moisture in food materials and therefore they are adversely reduced when foods are dehydrated.

Dehydrating foods started as far back as times when early men spread their harvests or hunts out in the sun for sun drying. It is one of the oldest methods of preservation, as the prehistoric men were fond of drying some seeds before planting.

In more recent times, American Indians stored their meats by laying them under the sun. The people of China also dried their eggs from the solar rays (sun shine) while their fellow Asian Japanese dried rice and fish under the sunrays. In the year 1975 however, the French made a major breakthrough in the development of Hot-air dehydration. Modern dehydration techniques have been largely stimulated by the advantages dehydration gives in compactness; on the average, dehydrated food has about 0.06667 the bulk of the original or reconstituted product.

During the Second World War, there was a great need to move food in bulk from place to place and this challenge ignited the developments of modern strategies on preserving foods, hence dehydration. The advantages of reduced bulk later came to be appreciated by campers and backpackers and also by relief agencies that provide food in times of emergency and disaster.

Dehydrating foods have a long heritage. The equipment for Dehydration differs in forms. Different food products have their equipment of dehydrations and these include tunnel driers, kiln driers, cabinet driers, vacuum driers, and other forms. Compact equipment suitable for home use is also available. A basic aim of design is to shorten the drying time, which helps retain the basic character of the food product. Drying under vacuum is especially beneficial to fruits and vegetables. Freeze-drying benefits heat-sensitive products by dehydrating in the frozen state without intermediate thaw. Freeze-drying of meat yields a product of excellent stability, which on rehydration closely resembles fresh meat.

Milk producing industries are part of the largest processors of dehydrated food, producing quantities of whole milk, skim milk, buttermilk, and eggs. Many dairy products are spray dried—that is, atomized into a fine mist that is brought into contact with hot air, causing an almost instant removal of moisture content.

Dehydration of foods has also been put into large scale practice by spaghetti producing companies. They use it in processing vegetables. Dehydration is probably the oldest method of preserving foods in that line. The companies make use of the removal of water from vegetables in order to ensure food preservation.

Food dehydration is the process of reducing the level of food moistures into smaller levels in order to extend the lifespan of the food. It requires adding different forms of energy to the food.

Dehydration can also be referred as the process of removing water through evaporation from a solid or liquid food. The aim of this is to arrive at a solid material that has been sufficiently water-reduced.

Note that dehydration does not include mechanical pressing of liquid foods. In most cases, Hot-air is used to add heat to the food and to reduce its moisture.

Fish, meats and food plants have been preserved over the years by drying them in the sun or naturally spread in the desert heat across different desert areas.

Food dehydration involves the following processes;

1. Simultaneous transfer of mass and heat around the food.

2. The medium used in transferring energy around the food.

In the absence of Hot-air, food dehydration can also be practiced through the use of other gases that can help reduce the moisture in the food.

Food dehydration involves some objectives which would be discussed below;

Objectives of Food Dehydration

- Impacting a peculiar feature, such as a different crispiness and flavor, to a food product. An example is the transformation of maize to cereal.

- Shrinking the food material into smaller and more portable sizes to change their forms. Food materials - when the water has been reduced - become more portable and easily packaged for transportation. Examples are the draining and grinding of curry leaves, thymes seeds etc. into spices.

- Reducing the volume and the weight of the food. The volume of water poses a substantial addition to the volume and weight of the food, by reducing the water content, the weight and volume of the food particle is also reduced.

- The conversion of food meals to a different form that is more convenient for storage, packaging and easy transportation. A great example is the conversion of milk or dairies to dry powder. When these products get to the places of consumption, they are reconverted to the previous forms through the addition of water.

- The effect of water depression which leads to preservation of the nutrients and longevity of the nutrients.

Advantages and Disadvantages of Dehydration

There are several advantages of dehydrating food, although all food storage processes also have their disadvantages. We shall briefly examine some of these advantages and disadvantages.

Advantages

1. Extended Lifespan: When foods are dehydrated, they last longer because the moist is reduced and the dry food does not encourage the survival of bacteria. The absence of bacteria keeps food in good shape and this can last for as long as three months. When food items are dehydrated, they are sometimes converted into substances that can last a life time. Examples are spices such as cinnamon and curry powder which is derived from the dehydration and grinding of curry leaves. In most cases, spices like this can last for several years without

2. Waste Reduction: When foods spoil, they reduce the amount of food available for consumption. Some food preservative methods usually give very short extension before spoilage of food. In many cases when we buy raw materials in the markets, the ability and knowledge to store them in good conditions help us keep the foods for a long time. This saves us a lot of stress and increases our income. Dehydrating our foods helps extend the lifespan of food for a long time.

3. Improvement in Food Tastes: The application of heat to reduce the water tastes in foods brings out the original taste of the other constituents of the food. The process of dehydration greatly improves the taste of food. When foods are water-filled, they are sometimes tasteless or acrid. When fruits are dried, the real taste is felt. In most cases, food tastes better when they are dehydrated.

4. Easy Storage: The fact that dehydrating foods make them easy to be stored is a great advantage of the process. When large bulks of foods are preserved in smaller packages – like the case of milk dehydrated into powder, it aids transportation and storekeeping. Through dehydration, storage is easier as it takes up lesser spaces.

5. Preservation of Nutrients: Dehydrating food maintains the nutrients in the food before they are dehydrated. Nutrients such as minerals, vitamins and enzymes are absolutely preserved during dehydration. Dehydration is only method that can ascertain the preservation of nutrients in food particles. Cooking and other preservative methods often lead to loss of nutrients. The entire essence of consuming food is to get benefits from the nutrients, if these nutrients are reduced; the essence of consuming the food has been lost.

6. Absence of Chemicals: The only substance needed to dehydrate food is the heat added to the food material. Unlike some other preservative methods, it does not involve the addition of chemicals. Dehydrating food therefore makes it safe from the fear of consuming poisonous substances because nothing but heat is added. The dehydrated food will only maintain its initial nutrients and that makes it perfect for consumption.

7. Economic and Financial Advantages: Dehydrating food makes food last longer and maintains the nutrient. In saving the food nutrients, it becomes easier to purchase such foods in large bulks. Usually, large bulk purchases always come at attractive discounts.

For several companies, the ability to maintain the nutrients of food despite their preservation has led to massive investment in such goods. Companies dehydrate dairy products and transport them over long distances where such products are needed. In the destination of these products, consumers pay heavily for purchasing the goods and this makes profitable yield for the investors.

8. Reliable for Emergency Situations: Dehydrating keeps a person prepared for any emergency that requires immediate need for dehydrated food. On a regular day, most people do not eat in between their sleeps, but in a situation where one suddenly wakes hungry in the middle of the night; such person can easily fetch dehydrated food in the house and get satisfied.

Disadvantages

1. Time Consumption: Dehydrating food requires a lot of time in order to achieve perfect results. Some food content have invisible water content, to reduce the water will require several time consumption and meticulous observation. Expelling such amount of time may be inconvenient to an individual.

2. Unwanted Addition of Weight: Dehydrated food is rich in calories and a satisfying quantity of the sweet meal leads to addition of weight for the consumer. Since the dehydrated content have shrink in size, they appear small, a little quantity consumed seemed insufficient while a large quantity consumed implies large nutrient consumption. The excess calories in the dehydrated food are the major cause of weight gain.

3. Dismissal of Nutrient: Dehydrating food can lead to loss of nutrients in the food. Some nutrients can't stand high levels of heat. The degree of heat applied therefore determines the survival of the nutrients in food. If the dehydrated food is not stored properly too, nutrient can be lost due to excess heat and poor storage condition.

4. Change in Taste and Look: With high heat, the appetizing appearances of common meals change. In most cases, people are easily turned off when foods don't wear the expected looks. When foods are dehydrated, the loss of water makes it shrink and the looks drastically change.

5. Technical Knowledge: Since not all foods are dehydrated in the same way or following the same pattern, dehydrating requires technical knowledge in order to be carried out well. There is also the place of experience which gradually makes a person perfect in the art.

Considering the above advantages and disadvantages, one would see how efficient it is to dehydrate foods. Although dehydrating foods has a lot more advantages than stated above, it is clearly the most effective method of food storage as it yields economical and financial advantages.

Why is Dehydration healthy?

Dehydration is healthy for consumption because of the following reasons:

1. Retains Nutrients: When we dehydrate foods, the nutrient in

the food is our primary concern. Unlike other methods of preservation, dehydration saves the nutrients in the dehydrated food when effectively it is carried out.

2. Bacteria free: Dehydrated foods are germ-free. When we keep these foods for a long period of time, they still maintain their healthy state.

3. No Addition of External Chemicals: The heat used to dehydrate food is the only external requirement for the process. This heat contains no chemicals or acids that may be dangerous for the food. Unlike some preservative methods which engage the addition of preservative chemicals, dehydration is a healthy choice for storing food.

4. Safe Handling: Since dehydration has nothing to do with handling dangerous chemicals or intense equipment, it is safe for the user to easily dehydrate. Dehydration can be done with the simplest household mechanical devices like oven, microwave or a dehydrator. The smoke or steam that escapes from dehydrating food is not unhealthy to the environment, unlike regular burning of waste products. This makes the process healthy.

Methods of Dehydration

Dehydration involves the following methods;

1. **Drum drying:** Foods like fish and other small animals that requires whole rinsing are dehydrated with the aid of a drum dryer. Drum drying is used to dry out the liquids from raw materials

dehydrated. It involves the use of low temperature in high capacity drums with an overlaying metal sheet. The dehydrated foods are layered on the sheets and the water is gradually evaporated from the heat.

In more recent times, drum drying retains the color and nutritional values of the dehydrated foods.

Advantages of Drum Drying

i. Drum dryers can be reused over a period of time.

ii. Cleaning drum dryers makes it easy to use and maintain.

iii. Drum dryers can heat up foods that are not easily dried with other methods of dehydration.

iv. Drum dryers are used for starches, fish, cereals, and potatoes, etc.

Disadvantages of Drum Drying

i. If not properly cleaned, particles from old dehydrated foods may stain and contaminate a new set of foods for dehydration.

ii. It may be difficult to clean the metal sheet because of the oily stains that may smear with it.

iv. Heat usually creates dark stains around materials used for the process.

2. **Microwave Vacuum Dryer:** This is an electric microwave that provides heats to food by making electro-magnetic radiation available for it in the frequency range. Microwave vacuum dryers

are oven-like and they make food heat up efficiently. These are commonly used in various kitchen and they are popular for warming previously cooked food or cooking some simple foods like pop corns etc. These vacuum driers are also used in slowly applying heat to slow-heated required food which easily gets burnt when cooked in pots and pans. Examples of foods cooked with these microwaves are; Margarines, hot butter, fats etc.

Advantages of Microwave Vacuum Dryer

i. Microwave vacuum driers are available in most homes and are easily accessed for use.

ii. They are used for various purposes including dehydrating, warming food and cooking.

Disadvantages of Microwave Vacuum Dryer

i. Microwave vacuum dryer cannot be used for oily foods such as bacon. If used, the speckles of the food attach itself to the microwave and can be difficult to remove.

ii. Improper use of the microwave may cause burns on the food intended for dehydration and in such case, the food may not have a well penetrated heating time.

3. Iyophilisation or Cryodesiccation: This is also called Freeze Drying. It is a dehydration process that requires low heat. It involves first of all freezing the product and then gradually lowering the pressing and finally getting rid of the ice through sublimation. The unique feature of this process is that unlike others which engage

heat, this uses ice.

Advantages of Iyophilisation or Cryodesiccation

i. It results in a high quality effect; this is due to the application of low temperature involved while dehydrating.

2. Freeze drying does not tamper with the shape or texture of the dehydrated food.

3. The taste and quality of the dehydrated food is greatly improved after it has been oven dried.

Stages in Iyophilisation

Iyophilisation involves four basic stages, they are; Pretreatment, Freezing, Primary Drying and Secondary Drying.

Pretreatment is the first stage, it involves all the methods used in treating the food before it freezing. These methods involve revision of the formulation, reducing its high vapor, and concentrating the food.

The second stage after the Pretreatment is the Freezing. This stage involves a cooled material below its triple point. It reaches the lowest temperature in which the states of matter can stay together. This phase is the most critical in the process of Iyophilisation or freeze drying. This stage can affect the rate of reconstitution, the time the cycle is complete and the stability of the food dehydrated.

The next stage – the Primary Drying stage involves lowering the pressure of the food dehydrated and supplying enough heat for the melting of the ice. Here, the heat is created chiefly by the radiation or conduction. At this stage, most of the water in the food is slowly dried off. This stage is usually slow because the heat is at a balance where it cannot be increased or decreased. If the heat is increased, the shape of the food will be affected.

The last stage of Iyophilisation is the Secondary drying. It is at this stage that the water content is completely removed. It involves raising the heat more than the previous stage. The essence of the increased heat is to destroy any interaction that has been created between water contents and the ice.

At the end of a successful process, the water content remaining in the food is usually below 1% to 3.9%.

Among all drying techniques, Iyophilisation produces the highest quality of result. It is expensive but it is one of the best methods because the structure of the food is completely maintained as well as the initial flavors.

4. Spray Drying: This is the conversion of food materials to a dry powder. It involves the use of drying product with a hot gas and converting them into liquid or slurry products. It is a common method of drying, acceptable for use in foods and pharmaceutical products. Spray driers use different atomizers or spray nozzles to disperse the liquid or slurry into a controlled drop sized spray.

5. Sun Drying: Sun drying is the earliest method of dehydration and it is still in practice till date in some countries and deserts. It involves spreading food materials under the intense heat from the sun. Foods that are sundried usually maintain the tastes and can last

effectively for a long period of time.

Sun drying is efficient for products like fish, meats and some solid dairy products. In some climes, sun dried products are half cooked and when ready for consumption, they are only further partially cooked and consumed. Sun drying can greatly improve the taste of the food while it makes it more nourishing.

Advantages of Sun Drying

1. Sun drying involves no equipment or fire. It makes use of natural sunlight for drying.

2. It saves energy and costs and makes food last longer.

3. It improves the taste and nutrients of food.

Disadvantages of Sun Drying

1. In some areas, fleas and insects can perch on the food when open to the environment.

2. If not properly done, the heating process may not be intense and the food may not be well dehydrated.

CHAPTER 2
DEHYDRATION AND OTHER METHODS OF FOOD PRESERVATION

To preserve food, as earlier explained, is to save the food for future use. The essence of preservation is to ensure that the saved food is kept in a good state. Losing the nutrient through the preservative measure is therefore synonymous to poor preservation. In this chapter, we shall examine various methods of food preservations in comparison to dehydration.

Food preservation is commonly regarded as the entire process of redeeming food and avoiding it from spoilage or decay. It involves storing food in a good condition for further consumption in the future. It keeps food nutritious, edible and maintains its quality.

Every attempt to prevent the spread of microorganisms, fungi and bacteria from infecting the food is known as preservation. Reducing the oxidation of fats to beat down rancidity is also a part of preservation.

While the color, texture and quality of food are never lost due to preservation, the end of a good preservation process should also ensure that the color of the food should be maintained. The preserved food is protected from pathogenic contaminants or chemicals.

There are various methods of Preservations, each one has its own advantages and disadvantages. In the next few pages, we shall examine these methods, effects and defects. They include the following:

1. **Increased Pressure:** This involves the compression of foods in a vessel. It involves exerting the weight of 70,000 – 90,000 pounds per square inch. The process kills microorganisms and truncates their growth. It does not alter the color, appearance or taste of the food.

Advantages:

i. It renders some enzymes deactivated.

ii. It leads to the destruction of microorganisms.

Disadvantage:

i. Nutrients that cannot endure heat are greatly lost.

2. <u>Jugging:</u> This is used especially for meats. It involves stewing the meats in an earthenware jugs or casserole. The meat is usually stewed with brine or wine. In some cases, the blood of the animal can also be used to stew the meat.

Advantages

i. The nutrient can be greatly increased and the food so preserved is richer.

ii. Meats preserved through this method last long without losing nutrients.

Disadvantage

i. This method leads to change of the taste of the food preserved.

3. **Bottling and Canning:** Canning is the process of sealing foods in sterile bottles and cans. When about to be consumed, the can with the food content is boiled in order to kill the microorganism in the can. Canned food must be kept sealed to keep the nutrients intact; any opening (irrespective of how small) will lead to infestation of the food by bacteria and inevitably spoilage.

Advantage: It can lead to the destruction of some microorganism and some enzymes.

Disadvantage: Water-soluble nutrient can be lost into liquid in cans or bottles.

4. **Jellying:** This is the process of preserving food through cooking the food in substances that converts the food into a gel. It is a good way of preserving fruits. Examples of fruits that can be preserved by the jellying methods include marmalades and cherry. The jellying aider is pectin and the addition of sugar.

Advantages:

i. The conversion leads to a sweeter taste.

ii. The process makes the food or fruit more nourishing.

Disadvantage:

i. Since people are accustomed to a pattern and look of food, the change in food appearance can be misinterpreted and unwanted in several circumstances.

5. **Pickling and Curing:** Pickling and Curing can also be referred to as Salting. It involves the application of salts to food. This application must be meticulously done for effective result. Salt reduces the activity of microorganisms in foods by 20% and sometimes even kills them. Salt also reduces the water from food such as meat. Pickling involves preserving through soaking food particles in saline water or other salt solution. It can also be the process of marinating the food in acetic acids, commonly known as vinegar.

Pickling can be categorized into fermentation pickling and chemical pickling. Both categories are effective depending on the food class the user intends to preserve.

Advantages

i. Salting keeps microbes away for as long as is needed.

ii. The shape, texture and size of the food remain intact.

Disadvantages:

i. Salting affects the taste of the food.

ii. Prolonged salting will change the color of the food.

6. Freezing: To freeze a food is to keep the food in cold store after preparation. Any natural or mechanical means of keeping the food in an atmospheric condition that is of very low temperature is freezing. Freezing is best for such food as Tomatoes, Potatoes and Pepper. In some very cold climes, people get warmed against the

overpowering cold but expose their food to the cold atmosphere for proper freezing and preservation.

Advantages:

i. It prevents microbial growth through its reduced temperature and lack of water molecules.

ii. It is a good method of retaining nutrients.

Disadvantages:

i. Blanching vegetables before freezing can lead to loss of the vitamins.

ii. Thawing unintentionally often leads to quality loss.

7. Drying: Drying is sometimes also referred to as dehydration but there is a distinct difference. It is the oldest method and it involves the process of reducing the amount of water present in a food. The removal of water prevents the spread of microorganisms such as bacteria and fungi and keeps the food safe. A good advantage of drying is that it shrinks the food and makes it easier to carry. Drying never reduces the quality or taste. The major necessities for drying are sun and wind. In more recent times; ovens drying, freeze drying, spray drying, commercial food dehydrators and bird dryers have gained prominent use.

Drying is the best method for preserving foods like fruits, meats and apples, etc.

Advantages:

i. Drying can produce concentrated food.

ii. Nutrients are almost totally retained.

iii. It inhibits autolytic enzymes and microbial growth.

Disadvantage:

i. Some nutrients can be lost in the process.

ii. Thiamines and Vitamin C are usually lost.

iii. Sulphur dioxide can be added to some fruits in order to keep the vitamins in it. Some people are allergic to Sulphur dioxide and in this case, it is harmful to them.

8. Chemical Preservation: This is the addition of preservative chemicals also known as preservatives to a food substance. For fruits like banana, orange and papaya etc., toxins can help ripen them early. The addition of preservatives make these foods last longer.

Some companies use preservative chemicals to extend the life-span of the products or food produced.

The essence of using preservatives is usually to keep food meant for export safe for the rigor of the journey and the time space before they reach the final consumers.

Advantages:

i. It leads to the death of microbes and bacteria.

ii. Nutrients are safe, none is loss.

Disadvantages:

i. The added chemicals are dangerous for some people's health.

9. Burial Preservation: In a place where there is abundance of land space, foods can be neatly buried for preservation. The absence of light and oxygen makes the acidity in the soil low. These features in addition to the coolness of the dark ground preserves cabbages and root vegetables.

Advantages:

i. Low acidity makes the preserved food intact.

ii. The preserved food is safely kept from burglary attacks or theft.

Disadvantages:

i. Nocturnal microorganisms can burrow into the soil and infest the food.

ii. In waterlogged areas, the preserved food may become damaged due to heat and moist.

10. Pulse Electric Field Processing: This is a new method of storing food which involves the strong electric field from brief pulses to process cells. The process is still under experiment. Crops that cannot be easily preserved can be collected in sealed bags with reduced concentration of oxygen in good atmosphere with high carbon dioxide. This is one of the best method preserving beers and wine.

Advantage:

i. Beers and Wines kept with this method can last for decades without changing taste and appearance.

Disadvantage:

i. It is difficult and expensive to construct.

11. **Fat Sealing Pot or Potting:** This process originated from Britain. It is used especially for meat. The process involves placing the food substance in a pot and sealing the pot with a layer of fat.

Advantage:

i. The fat layer prevents the penetration of microbes and fungi.

Disadvantage:

i. The process cannot be used for a very long period of time.

12. Radiation of Ions: This involves the radiation of ion content in food to preserve the food from getting spoilt. It is good for fruits that are processed for the purpose of exportation.

Advantages:

i. It changes the flavors of sterilized foods into better aroma.

ii. It extends the lifespans of some mushroom and berries.

iii. It inhibits sprouting potatoes.

Disadvantages:

i. Extended life of fruits leads to diminished nutrients.

ii. Preserved fruits are not as delicious and nutritious as freshly plucked and eaten fruits.

13. **Vacuum Packing:** This process involves the creation of a vacuum by building air tight bags and bottles. When the air is tight, the bacteria and microorganism cannot survive because – like other animals, the microorganisms will be unable to breathe and will eventually die. Vacuum packing is best for fruits – especially when the fruit is dry.

To use this process, the user must ensure that no air gets into the space created because microorganisms need very little air to breathe. Once there is a little space, the contaminants will breathe easily. The ability of contaminants to breathe within the space invalidates the process.

Advantages:

i. Air-tight content keeps microorganisms off the space and can preserve food for very long periods.

Disadvantages:

i. Once opened, the process must be restarted to remain valid. Fetching fractions of the preserved food is therefore not possible.

14. Smoking: Smoking is the process of heating up food through the use of smokes from exposed burning woods. No microorganism can endure the intensity of the smoke that is emitted from the

burning wood and they therefore dry up in the process of smoking.

Smoking is best applied to fish or meat. Over the years there has been a great advancement in the development of smoking processes. The development includes; cold smoking, smoke baking, hot smoking and etc.

By preserving food through smoking, the risk of cancer is greatly increased.

Advantages: It usually involves the incorporation of smoky substances and drying to keep the food safe.

Disadvantages: Smoking can cause cancer. In some parts of the world, it is regarded as pollution as they believe it leads to the emission of carbon which is toxic.

15. Sugar Coating: To make use of this process, sugar is first melted into syrup or crystallized. The syrup is used to store fruits. The crystalized form is applied through cooking the food in the sugar until crystallization occurs. The latter is best for ginger and candid peel.

Sugar coating can also be used for glazed fruit. Glazed fruit are coated in a superficial form with the syrup.

Many times, alcohol can be added to sugar to keep luxury food such as mixed fruits for cake and other baked products.

Advantages:

i. Coating with sugar disallows microbial growth.

ii. Sugar coating does not destroy the nutrients of the food.

Disadvantage:

i. Sugar taste is increased. Sometime, this can be unwanted by people who do not like sugar.

With the well analyzed methods of preservation above. We shall briefly examine the major difference between Drying and Dehydrating.

The two concepts have often been used interchangeably, but they differ technically and in basic application.

Difference between Drying and Dehydrating

Although both concepts can mean the same thing, the major difference between drying and dehydration is that Dehydration refers to the removal of water from the water-containing compound while Drying has to do with eradicating solvent from a solid, semi-solid or a liquid.

Drying is the process of removal of solvent from a solid, semi-solid or a liquid. Hence, it is a mass transfer process because the solvent mass in the solution moves from the solution to the atmosphere via drying. Here, the solvent can be water or any other solvent such as organic solvents. Also, this mass transfer occurs via evaporation. Often, we use this process as the final step before the packaging of some products. The final product of the drying process is always solid. It can be in continuous sheet form, in long pieces, particles or as a powder.

While we use advanced machines for dehydration, we use heat energy for the evaporation and for drying. We need an agent that can remove the solvent vapor produced from the evaporation. Desiccation, on the other hand, is a synonym for drying, but sometimes we consider it as an extreme of drying.

Dehydration and Drying both refer to the removal of solvent from a solution, thereby leaving only the solute. Therefore, both these processes are mass transfer processes. Moreover, these processes will leave a solid residue at the end.

There is a little difference in application. The applications of drying process are in the food industry, the pharmaceutical industry, etc. we can dry food items in order to inhibit microbial growth and thereby to preserve the food. Other than that, it also reduces the volume and the mass of the item. In addition to that, we dry non-food items such as wood, paper, washing powder, etc.

Drying is the process of removal of solvent from a solid, semi-solid or a liquid whereas dehydration is the removal of water from the water-containing compound. Therefore, this is the fundamental difference between drying and dehydration. Another important difference between drying and dehydration is that drying process produces water or any other solvent as the byproduct while dehydration produces water as an essential byproduct. Apart from that, we can use mild conditions without any control for drying purposes. But we have to control the conditions such as humidity and temperature for the dehydration purpose.

Both drying and dehydration processes are mass transfer processes. They involve in the removal of a solvent from a compound. They differ from each other according to "what" they are going to remove. Therefore, the key difference between drying and dehydration is that drying refers to the removal of solvent from a solid, semi-solid or a liquid whereas dehydration refers to the removal of water from the water-containing compound.

Despite the common misuse of both concepts, dehydrated foods are usually products of drying. Although not all dry foods are dehydrated. Some foods or fruits are dry from their growth. Good examples of such fruits are fruits grown in the desert.

CHAPTER 3
DEHYDRATING TECHNIQUES: HOW TO ACHIEVE BEST RESULTS

Dehydration is the best way to ensure that our diets are kept safe for future use. The major reasons why dehydrating food is better than other methods of preservations are; dehydration can be quickly and easily carried out. When compared to purchasing already dehydrated foods, dehydrating your own food domestically requires less cost. The end result of dehydrated food is always more delicious and nourishing. Nourishing foods make the consumer healthier and it leads to lesser wastes. Also, dehydrating your food saves space as the food becomes dry and lighter in weight. Getting a good dehydrator is not expensive, and when you think about its durability, you'd realize that it saves a lot. A good dehydrator cost is between sixty to seventy USD. Although if you are planning on getting one of the high-end devices such as an Excalibur, that can be a horse, but basically a common dehydrator can satisfy all your domestic dehydrating just as well.

It is important to consider these things you will need to know before purchasing or using your dehydrator. Knowing these things will serve as a guide to help you effectively use the device.

1. Check out the Manual: Every such device always come with a manual or handbook. Many times, people ignore reading the guidebook. But the essence of the guidebook is to give guidance to the buyer. Always read the manual of your devices.

Among all dehydrators, back fan dehydrators encourage even drying but it requires moving the trays to make sure the drying is really even. Dehydrators have three fans, the top fans, the back fan and the bottom fan.

2. Differences in Temperature: Different foods will require different dehydration temperatures. Check your dehydrator thermostat and make sure it is accurate before beginning to dry meat or fish. Also, always remember to clean your dehydrator between families of items, or between doing meat or fish and any fruit or veggie.

3. The Multipurpose Use of Dehydrators: You can also use your dehydrator to make special foods, like kale chips, for snacks or storage. If you are making something like kale chips, which have oil and spices on them, you will want to ensure the trays get washed before drying fruit or something that doesn't go well with garlic.

4. Dehydrating Fruits by making them into Puree is very effective: Fruit purees are an awesome way to store and eat overripe, funny shaped, or otherwise damaged fruits.

Small apples are awesome turned into fruit leather, and overripe plums, peaches, and berries also work amazing in fruit leather. You can combine most other fruits with apples to make flexible leather that is perfect for snacks and keeping on hand for emergency energy.

If you do not have a dedicated puree tray as an accessory with your dehydrator, it is very easy to cover the normal tray with some cello wrap and dry on that. However, if you are using cello wrap, always make sure to flip the leather once the top is dry so that it dries completely on both sides.

5. Improvising when Necessary: In the absence of a dehydrator, ovens or air dries can be used. Any leafy green–mint, lemon balm, sage, oregano, lettuce, or even carrot tops – can be air dried. Vegetables and herbs are particularly easy to dry. All you have to do is hang them up in a dry room. Depending on the size of your vegetable or herb, it can take anywhere from a few days to a week to fully dry. Vegetables and herbs should be crisply dried and should crumble easily. If you try this method, make sure direct sunlight does not strike the vegetables because it might perish under sunlight.

6. Only the same classes of food should be dehydrated together: Imagine laundering a bunch of different colored and different textured clothes in the same machine, catastrophic, right? The same thing applies to food. You should dehydrate foods that have the same classes together. If you are dehydrating tomatoes, you can also do hot peppers, but be aware that the tomatoes will end up being spicy. Any brassica should be dehydrated alone; otherwise the sulfur taste will permeate into the other foods. Fruits can be mixed together, but mixing them with strong tasting or smelling vegetables is not recommended. This is just like your laundry rules.

Irrespective of the dehydrating device you decide to use, you can always engage some tricks to ensure that the drying is well circulated within and around the food. Cut your vegetables, herbs and fruits into the same width or sizes in order to allow equal amount of heat circulate. Make sure also, that the pieces do not overlay one another. If there is an overlay, the heat will not penetrate into the space between the overlay. The exception is greens, as they are loose and dry easily even with a few light layers on the tray.

7. Multipurpose Dehydrators are best stored Cool: If you intend to dry hot peppers or onions, keep your dehydrator outside in a well-ventilated area.

And be prepared to scrub the dehydrator trays with soap and water afterward. With peppers, the oils will become airborne in the first part of the dehydrating process and can be an eye irritant. The oils will also remain on the trays, so take care when cleaning them and packing the dried peppers away.

Onions are more airborne than peppers, so make sure there is plenty of ventilation around the dehydrator when working with them.

8. The Trick with Dehydrating Berries: Berries, like blueberries or grapes, can be a challenge on the dehydrating front.

They are small, but a contained unit. Most berries are small enough to be dried whole, but large grapes should be cut in half. If you want to dry seeded grapes, you can cut them in half to remove the seeds and then dry them. Berries can easily over-dry, so you want to watch and make sure that they remain slightly supple, and not too crispy.

9. Vegetables, Fruits and Herbs can be dehydrated at any and every stage of development: Since dehydration will still the food at a stage and keep it in that stage for a long time, vegetables, fruits and herbs can be dehydrated irrespective of how ripe they are. If one of these is too ripe and soft, one can always make it into puree, and then dry the puree. Although using the best quality fruits and veggies will result in the best quality dried goods. The target is to make it last long in good conditions not to convert it into a perfect substance.

Have no fear in dehydrating bruised, overripe, and slightly damaged fruits. Simply endure that you do not put mold in the dehydrator. Molds can smear on the surface and cause quicker spoilage of the other food materials.

10. Procedures for Vegetables before Dehydration:

Blanching your vegetables before dehydration is a good thing. This is not very important but it will keep the colors intact and it will help retain the vitamins. With this, your dehydrated vegetable will taste fresher after you rehydrate it. All you have to do is lower your food into boiling water for a few minutes then put it in ice-cold water to stop it from cooking. Here's a guide to blanching vegetables.

With a dehydrator, you don't have to waste much of anything. One fun way to get the most out of your summer harvest, and your dehydrator, is to dry and powder items you'd normally get rid of. Have an over-abundance of late-season lettuce, chard, beet greens, or carrot tops? Dry them all and powder them in a food processor–

it makes an easy to store vitamin powder for late winter soups and stews.

If you're making tomato sauce, take the skins you'd normally throw away and dehydrate them. Then powder the skins and you have your own tomato powder that is perfect for mixing into sauces or breads. You can dry tomato skins and hot peppers at the same time if you want a spicy tomato powder. Storage is very important for any preserved food, and dehydrated foods are no exception.

Store either in heavy-duty zippered bags in a metal container, or store in dry, sterile, glass jars. If you choose to store in plastic bags within a larger can, keep food families separate.

For example, don't try to store the broccoli in the same can as peaches. If you do, each will pick up hints of flavor from the other, which wouldn't taste very good.

Knowing the techniques behind using equipment always makes the use of dehydrators more effective. A simple trick can make a whole lot of workload seem like a walk in the park. Techniques also aid us in avoiding accidents and burning our foods while attempting to dehydrate them. Another safety tip, as discussed earlier, is for users to thoroughly go through the manual that comes with their purchases. Certain conditions are palatable for the use of dehydrating equipment. Careless use might lead to unwanted circumstances and the only way to avoid them is to take safety precaution.

CHAPTER 4
IDEAL DEHYDRATING TEMPERATURE FOR VARIOUS FOODS AND FRUITS

Generally, foods are best dehydrated at 140°F. The use of higher temperature might turn the process into roasting or cooking. When food cooks externally without expelling its moisture, then case hardening will occur. A case hardening food will turn into molds and the dehydrating intention will be forfeited. This therefore explains that dehydration is impossible under very high dehydrating temperatures.

Dehydrating is aided also when the humidity is low. The essence of dehydration is to reduce the water content in the food. In order to achieve a complete dehydration process, the water content in the food must be evaporated into the atmosphere. If you dehydrate in a misty environment, much of the water that should escape the food will be replenished by the settling moist. To speed the drying time, ensure that the food is dehydrated in an environment that increases air flow.

To dehydrate food indoors, you will need modern food dehydrators, common ovens or counter top convectional ovens. Microwaves are usually used for dehydration but they should only be used for drying vegetables and herbs. The disadvantage of using microwaves for multipurpose dehydration is because there is no creation of a well aerated atmosphere for denser food.

When you want to dehydrate your vegetables, herbs and meats, you should avoid using outdoor methods because they are low in sugar and acids and the risk of spoiling the food intended dehydration is spoilt. Meats are high in protein, and all proteins encourage the growth of microbes and fungi. When heat is not properly controlled, the best method is to dehydrate your herbs, vegetables and meats indoors.

The essence is to control the environment. If given the appropriate atmospheric conditions, meats, herbs and vegetable can be dehydrated outdoor. This though will be done at great risk. It is best to dehydrate using the sun shine on hot and breezy days but these ideal conditions are not usually available in all areas.

The best foods to sun dry are foods that are rich in sugar and acid content. Sun drying requires several days to make foods dry. This is often because the level and intensity of sunshine is not humanly controlled. Outdoor dehydration requires a minimum temperature of 85°F is needed, but any temperature higher than that is all good too.

When dehydrating fruits with sun rays, ensure that you cover it well. After spreading collect the spread items when evening approaches because the cool night air condenses. Condensed air adds moisture to virtually everything.

When using Freezer method, make sure the food is sealed in freezer type plastic bags that are placed in a freezer. The freezer should be left for about two days with the temperature set at 0°F.

To use oven method, arrange the pieces of food neatly in the oven tray or in a shallow pan. Make sure you arrange them in a single layer. After layering, set the tray in an oven set to a temperature between 140°F to 160°F. Once done, allow the content to bake for thirty minutes. For air circulation, it is better to leave the door of the oven opened. A six inches opening is good. Ensure that the tray is not too wide, so that it can clear the sides of the oven and should be 4inches shorter than the oven from front to back.

Dehydrators have been built to extract water content from food quickly at 140°F. Users have to consistently check the following features;

1. A fan or a blower.

2. Enclosed Thermostat from 85°F to 160°F.

3. Double wall construction of metal or High Grade plastic. It is not often advisable to use wood because of the hazard it can cause. Wood is also difficult to clean.

4. A timer.

5. At least four open mesh trays. The trays must be made with plastic and must be sturdy in order to be washed easily.

Comparison between Oven Drying and Dehydrators

a. <u>Speed:</u> In terms of speed, oven drying is slower than dehydrators because it does not have a built in fan for the air movement. It takes twice or thrice longer when you dry food in an oven than when you dry it in a dehydrator.

b. **Energy consumption:** Oven drying consumes more energy than dehydrators. The rate of energy consumption is about thrice or four times the rate of dehydrators.

c. **Cost:** Dehydrators are more expensive than ovens of the same size. Ovens are multi-purposed and can be used for several other cooking and baking.

If well dehydrated, most dried fruits can be stored for a whole year given that they are exposed to 60°F. The fruits will last up to half of that if heated at 80°F.

To dry foods again at 140°F, the foods should be stored in the coolest areas of the home. Store them in areas with temperature below 70°F.

Foods should be pasteurized in ovens at 160°F. Make sure they heat up to 30 minutes.

Next, we shall observe the preparations for dehydration problem.

There are common problems we encounter when dehydrating, especially when using a dehydrator. Sometime, fright might cause us to feel like we have created a huge problem and that can be channels of making bigger mistakes.

If you come across any of the problems below, here are guides to solving them.

1. If you encounter the problem of molds on food, then take note of the following.

Causes: This is usually caused by not checking food regularly for the development of moisture (check this weekly), container not0020air tight, incomplete drying. This can also happen if the temperature for storage is too high and there is moisture in the food.

Prevention: Check containers regularly to watch out for moisture. The best prevention is to test pieces of the food for dryness. Always use air tight containers. Keep food in the coolest places around the home. Lastly, dehydrate food again at 140°F.

2. If you encounter the problem of brown spots on vegetables or some fruits, take note of the following.

Causes: This is caused when you have used too high temperature in dehydrating the vegetable or fruit.

Prevention: Always dry the vegetables and fruits at 140°F. Also, periodically check the dehydrated vegetables for dryness.

3. If you encounter the problem of moisture in the jar or container, take note of the following.

Causes: Uneven food cut, leaving dried food at room temperature for too long thereby allowing moisture to penetrate through again, and Incomplete drying.

Prevention: The best prevention is to cut food evenly from the beginning of the process. Also, test many of the pieces. Lastly, it is good to cook quickly and package the food, so that it does not stay unattended for too long.

4. In a case where you encounter insects in jars, then take note.

Causes: It is very likely that the foods were dried outdoors but were not pasteurized; it may also be that the lids used do not completely fit jars.

Prevention: Pasteurize foods in oven at a temperature that is not lower or higher than 160°F in ovens for thirty minutes. If you are using a freezer, pasteurize for 48 hours. Use new can lids that would perfectly fit.

5. If there are holes in plastic bags.

Causes: There is a hole in the bag; it is caused by insects or rodents biting through the bag.

Prevention: Do not use plastic bags unless you want to store the foods in the refrigerator.

CHAPTER 5
HEALTHY LIVING AND DIET TIPS

Health is the greatest wealth anyone can possess. To have a healthy life, it is important to maintain a balanced diet. A balanced diet is a diet that consist the accurate amount and proportion of food needed by the body to maintain healthy growth. It is a diet that provides all the nutrients the body needs to function properly. Consuming most of your daily calories from fresh fruits and vegetables will improve your healthy living.

Eating the right food in the right proportion can help consumer avoid a lot of diseases and health issues. A well balanced diet provides important vitamins, minerals and nutrients needed to keep the physical and mental parts of people strong and healthy.

Maintaining a balanced diet also helps prevents against excess weight and provides your body sleep better. The brain functions properly when the right food is consumed.

When you consume all the classes of food; fats and oil, proteins, carbohydrates, vitamins, minerals and water in the right proportion, then you are taking a balanced diet. Although for some people, due to historical records, they may need some classes of foods, such as vitamins more than they need some others, such as fats and oil. A person who has a history of excess weight or obesity may be recommended to consume less food with starch and fats and oil.

Averagely, everyone should take at least a portion of all the classes of food. It is safe to take note of the proportion taken to avoid damaging results.

Healthy living is not the only importance of taking a balanced diet. Let's examine some other importance below;

1. Building up intelligence: Consuming fruits with healthy acids builds the consumer's intelligence. Omega III fatty acid improve intelligence and allows the brain open to learn more easily. It also fights against disorders, dementias and other mental conditions.

2. Deep and Better Rest: Normal sleeping is supposed to invigorate the sleeper. It should freshen up the body system upon waking, but it is only when one consumes balanced diet that one can truly feel relieved in this manner. Eating proper diets renders quick recoveries from the day's stress when one rests. Without proper sleep, you can feel dizzy after waking due to low energy level. The evidence of the low energy is sluggish feeling and affected focus level.

Improper diet intake strains the nerve and makes good sleep difficult. Over eating, which is also a form of improper diet consumption, can lead to indigestion or digestive distress. It is extremely difficult for the body to rest well when it is also saddled with the responsibility of digesting a large amount of calories. If you often experience discomfort when you sleep, then it may be due to improper diet consumption.

3. Combating Illnesses and Diseases: A proper intake of balanced diet will energize the antibodies and hemoglobin which help fight against germs in the immune system. Insufficient intake of some classes of food will reduce the amount of nutrient consumed and that can lead to impairment. Consuming vitamins, zinc and iron improve vascular activities.

The consumption of vegetables and fruits increases the strength of white blood cells which fight against diseases in the body. They also lead to the production of bacterial preventing aids that stops bacteria from habiting the body.

Fruits are rich in vitamin C. Vitamin C lowers blood pressure and raises the level of good cholesterol. It also debars the conversion of fats into plaques in the arteries. Veins are responsible for transporting blood to the heart and arteries transport blood from the heart.

4. Energy Provider: Proteins like milk, meat and eggs, in proper consumption will give the body the necessary amount of energy. Food that is rich in iron such as vegetable always boosts the energy. Balanced diet provides energy for the body for a long period of time. When you consume foods that easily digest however, the body digests the food quickly, giving room for a quicker hunger. Such food will lead to excessive eating which can damage the digestive system. Balanced diet provides sufficient energy to carry on with the day's activity having the amount of energy needed.

5. Weight Balance: Eating junks often leads to excessive weight

gain. Excessive weight gain may lead to absence of self-esteem. Healthy eating helps maintain attractive shape and desired weight. Although exercises can also help you keep in good shape, such exercise can work best when accompanied by a well eaten balanced diet.

Of course, eating a balanced diet is not the only tip that would transform you into the perfect or most healthy individual. Other tips are needed, and below are a list of things that you can do to live perfectly healthy.

The requirements for healthy living cannot all be contained in a compendium, but the maximum anyone can do is to highlight relevant points. Therefore, these points do not exhaust the requirement. They are:

1. **Eat Varieties of Fruits and Vegies:** Taking vegetables and fruits of different colors and vitamins will provide sufficient nutrients for your health. Berries and pepper of all colors are very beneficial to your health. Take juices that are naturally made too for sufficient vitamins.

2. **Feed to Mental Balance:** What we eat is a direct representation of who we become. Careless eating gives an apparent reflection on the outlook while a balanced diet also reflects a balanced lifestyle.

3. **Consume Sufficient Nutrients:** Provide the necessary amount your body needs by consuming different choices of foods that contains nutrients such as whole grains, milk, fruits, low fats and

vegetables. Eating fat-free food will also provide nutrients to your body. Reduce the number of salt you take because sodium foods damage the health.

4. **Drink a lot of Water:** Some scientists declare that water cannot be taken in excess as long as the body has space for it. Water flushes away waste products from the body and it keeps the body regulated. Rather than taking carbonated drinks and soda, water intake is of very great benefits. Rather than other drinks that have sugary content, simply spice your water with a slice of lemon, lime, apple or fresh mints or basils.

You need plenty fluids to fight dehydration. Scientists recommend six to eight glasses of water daily. The glasses of water are an addition to the food eaten. Wines that are not alcoholic, beverages and juices also counts as water.

5. **Include Sea food in your meals:** Omega III fatty acid is good for you and it is richly embedded in sea food. Protein and minerals are also constituents of sea food. It is good that adult eats not less than eight ounces of sea food every week. Children may eat about four to five ounces weekly. Examples of fish food from sea are; Trout, Salmon, Shellfish (Mussels, Oysters and Crabs), and Tuna.

6. **Watch the Sizes of Food You Eat:** When you are cooking, serve the meals in smaller plates in order to check the size you consume. Avoid habits like licking up the plates and getting quick snacks after meals. Portion sizes should depend on the age, gender and activity level.

7. **Cut Down on Commonly Abused Food:** Fats, salt and sugar are commonly abused by being consumed in carless quantities. Read labels on packaged ingredients to discover food with reduced salts. Drink water always in place of sweet drinks. When cooking, reduce the quantity of salt you cook with. Herbs and spices are good replacements. Examples of spices are garlic, onions, turmeric, ginger etc.

Sugary food increases the risk of obesity and tooth decay. More than 22.5g of the total sugar per 100g implies a high level of sugar. 5g of total sugar per 100g implies that the food is low in sugar. Scientists say that eating in smaller plates will encourage you to eat less. Using bigger plates creates the notion within you that you haven't eaten enough. Also, according to research, eating in plates which has contrasting colors to the food discourages overeating.

Excessive salt consumption can lead to high blood pressure and goiter. Use the guide on food labels to cut down on your salt intake. More than 1.5g of salt per 100g implies that the sodium level is much.

8. **Boost Your Muscle:** Eating food that contains proteins will help you build your body tissues and muscles. Beef, pork, milk and eggs are rich in protein but in several cases they have a lot of fats along with them. It is advisable to reduce the fats by taking low fat cuts of beef and pork, skinless chicken or turkey will help reduce the fats. Plant based protein foods such as soy beans, peas and nuts contain less fat.

9. **Use whole grain flour in baking recipes:** There are brans in whole grain flour and this makes it more nourishing in baked diets. Examples are oat meal, pasta, brown rice and whole wheat bread.

10. **Cut Down on Saturated Fats:** Always pay attention to the type and quantity of fats that you consume. The two main types of fats are; Saturated and Unsaturated fats. When consumed in excess, saturated fats can boost the quantity of cholesterol in the blood; the effect is an increase in the development of heart diseases. While children should eat just about 5-10g of fats in a day, women should consume 20g of saturated fats in a day while men should consume 30g in a day. Children who are under the age of five are advised against taking fats.

Foods that have saturated fats are butter, meats, sausage, pies, lad and biscuits.

Unsaturated fats are healthy for all ages, they include; vegetable oils, oily fish and avocadoes. All types of fats are high in energy. Fats should only be eaten in small amount.

11. **Do not skip Breakfast:** A healthy breakfast is the most important meal of the day. It should be high in fiber and low in fats and oil. Sugar and salt can be a part of a balanced diet. A low whole grain lower sugar cereal with semi skimmed milk and a fruit slice is a perfect breakfast.

Healthy living cannot be complete if one fails to mention and reemphasize the importance of exercises. While the topic of exercise may seem inconsequential, the level of comfort we sometimes experience makes it increasingly distant engagement. Modern development of super-comfort facilities like remote controls, lifts, social media entertainment etc. have aided lack of regular exercises.

To avoid the ills of refusing to engage in daily exercises, we shall examine the topic of exercises.

Exercises, Comfort and Diet Tips

To achieve a healthy lifestyle, exercise must be a major part of your life. Lack of exercises is a direct cause of consistent weaknesses, obesity and short endurance. One of the major ills of lack of exercise is also sickness. By exercising daily, the practice can help increase self-esteem and self-confidence, decrease stress and anxiety, enhance mood, and improve general mental health. Regular exercise can help control body weight and in some people cause loss of fat. Thirty minutes of modest exercise at least 3 to 5 days a week is also recommended, but the greatest health benefits come from exercising most days of the week.

You can breakdown your exercises into short routine of just fifteen to twenty minutes daily. Start slowly and progress gradually to avoid injury or excessive soreness or fatigue. Over time, increase the time to thirty to fifty minutes of moderate to vigorous exercise every day.

There is never an age where you should stop exercising. You are never too old to start exercising. Even frail, elderly individuals who can still move their bodies can improve their strength and balance with exercise. Make sure you exercise ever mobile part of your body.

Tips to Daily Exercise

1. Daily exercises as simple as moderate physical activities can help avoid over relaxation of the muscles. While engaging in daily exercises, ensure that you are not experiencing pains while working out.

2. Learn and faithfully practice simple acrobatics. Yoga is also a good way to keep the body in good shape. Although there is no scientific benefit of yoga other than the regular benefits of exercise. Those who practice yoga have a physical and mental balance.

3. Rather than taking easy or convenient routes to achieving your goals, try going through the strenuous route. If your office is in a sky scraper building, reduce the height of elevators. Deliberately take the staircase in order to burn accumulating fats around the thighs and joints.

4. While exercising, stretch your body to their extremes. Be sure to stay hydrated and eat foods that contain a meaningful quantity of protein, especially after your exercise. Proteins keep the muscles strong.

5. Set aside two to three hours weekly for exercises. For medium intensity exercises, try a three hours routine every week. Spend two hours for high intensity exercise weekly.

6. Engage in aerobics as well as mixed sports. Try different sports and exercised that puts different parts of your body and joints into activeness. Consistent practice will trigger the production of

endorphins which makes you feel happy and positive.

7. Good diets work hand in hand with good exercise routine. It expels the possibility of weaknesses and alleviates your wellbeing. Eating fiber can elongate satisfaction and hunger wouldn't be a consistent feeling. Sticking to an exercising routine will help your body burn calories.

To live healthy goes beyond physical healthiness. Healthy living has to do with mental and emotional balances as well. While it is good to learn all that is needed for positive living, it is also important to learn how to avoid unhealthy lifestyles.

There is a close connection between a person's physical and mental health. Once you live physically healthy, it will have a direct reflection on your mental balance too. In the next few paragraphs too, I shall discuss tips on how to attain meaningful emotional health.

As indicated earlier, not all classes of food is to be consumed in the same proportion by everyone. Human beings have different nutritional requirement because of their different ages and hereditary tendency.

The older you get, the more the quantity of food you eat and the spaces between meals becomes longer. Children, on the other hand may eat at an interval of up to four hours daily while adults may stick to the three meals per day routine.

Some foods are not limited to specific ages. Examples of such are simple snacks. Snacks can be taken every now and then without a regular time space.

Eating three times a day – breakfast, lunch and dinner, is an ideal principle. Some adults however make the error of assuming that their dinner should be the biggest meal. Heavy dinner is responsible for digestive distress because the digestive systems are overworked.

What is important is to consume healthy foods which include whole grains, vegetables, low fat and oils. Add lean meats, poultry, fish, beans, eggs, and nuts into a healthy diet.

Choose foods that are low in saturated fats, trans fats, cholesterol, salt (sodium), and added sugars; look at the labels because the first listed items on the labels comprise the highest concentrations of ingredients.

Control portion sizes; eat the smallest portion that can satisfy hunger and then stop eating.

Healthy snacks are good in moderation and should consist of items like fruit, whole grains, or nuts to satisfy hunger and not cause excessive weight gain.

Avoid sodas and sugar-enhanced drinks because of the excessive calories in the sodas and sugar drinks; diet drinks may not be a good choice as they make some people hungrier and increase food consumption. Avoid eating a large meal before sleeping to decrease gastroesophageal reflux and weight gain.

It is always hard to control your weight when you have already attained an enormous weight size. Check your weight regularly to keep a balance. Eating food that would boost your weight or size may seem initially as a harmless venture

If you are expressing depression or trying to overcome anger, consuming food in heavy sizes is the biggest harm you can do to yourself. Some people express their anger by aggressively eating much; this will only make the problem worse.

Many adults who find it difficult to resist excessive consumption of sugary products become addicted to it by being lured with petty sugary gifts. You should avoid offering people gifts that contains sugar because you may be doing them more harm than good when you offer them such. Sugar may cause diabetes; this is why scientists recommend that it should be taken in low quantity.

It is healthy to stay away from heavy meals, especially during summer. Experience makes it clear that heavy food increases the discomfort within us when we eat such in hot weather.

If you are a vegan or vegetarian, then you should constantly visit your doctor regularly. Breaking regular consultation with your doctor might have you lose out on healthy food update. A vegetarian lifestyle has been promoted for a healthy lifestyle and weight loss; vegetarians should check with their doctors regularly to be sure they are getting enough vitamins, minerals, and iron in their diet.

If you are trying to lose some body fat, then you should avoid all fatty and sugary foods. Let your focus be mainly on vegetables, fruits, and nuts and markedly reduce your intake of meat and dairy products. These would only increase your weight and size.

Meats especially need to be well cooked or heated. Avoid eating raw or undercooked meats of any type.

If you are diabetic, constantly check your glucose levels as directed; try to keep the daily blood glucose levels as close to normal as possible. Remember that your life depends on how well you attend to your welfare.

Heating your food well enough can kill all bacteria in foods. Make sure the temperature is close to 170°F. This destroys most harmful bacteria and other pathogens; if you choose to eat uncooked foods like fruits or vegetables, they should be thoroughly washed with running treated tap water right before eating. Washing your fruits keeps you safe from a lot of contagious diseases.

People with unusual work schedules (night shifts, college students, military) should try to adhere to a breakfast, lunch, and dinner routine with minimal snacking.

If you have a history of body odor, avoid foods with flour contents. Flour triggers sweats. When bacteria perch on the sweats, they excrete on the skin. Within a few moments, the sweat becomes smelly and produces the body odor that turns people off.

Since addiction to food can be very convulsive behavior, you may need to seek medical advice early if you cannot control your weight, food intake, or if you have diabetes and cannot control your blood glucose levels. Regular exercise can help you as a safe first measure.

Keep the body agile by working out and exercising. This will prevent and reverse age-related decreases in muscle mass and strength, improve balance, flexibility, and endurance, and decrease the risk of falls in the elderly. Regular exercise can help prevent coronary heart disease, stroke, diabetes, obesity, and high blood pressure. Regular, weight-bearing exercise can also help prevent osteoporosis by building bone strength.

Regular fitness can help chronic arthritis sufferers improve their capacity to perform daily activities such as driving, climbing stairs, and opening jars.

Almost any type of exercise (resistance, water aerobics, walking, swimming, weights, yoga, and many others) is helpful for everybody. Children need exercise; play outside of the home is a good beginning.

Sports for children may provide excellent opportunities for exercise, but care must be taken not to overdo certain exercises (for example, throwing too many pitches in baseball may harm a joint like the elbow or shoulder).

Exertion during strenuous exercise may make a person tired and sore, but if pain occurs, stop the exercise until the pain source is discovered; the person may need to seek medical help and advice about continuation of such exercise. Most individuals can begin moderate exercise, such as walking, without a medical examination.

Early knowledge about living healthy is as good as living healthy. It is imperative to train your kids in the positive light that you have learnt. Tomorrow starts today and early commitment to healthy living will prolong your lifespan.

RECIPES

HOW TO DEHYDRATE AND USE VEGETABLES, MEAT AND.... MUCH MORE

Lots dry fruit because it makes a really healthy snack, but when it comes to using a food dehydrator to preserve food, it's more common to dry vegetables instead. So if this is your end goal, to store your summer-grown food for later, then you'll likely be dealing in veggies sooner or later.

Basic technique:

Don't know how to dehydrate vegetables? Drying vegetables is basically like drying any other type of food. Wash everything thoroughly, peel off any rinds or inedible skin, and slice up your veggies in evenly sized pieces. Thin slices work best, especially for heavy or thick foods. Try for between 1/4 and 1/8 of an inch. Something like carrot could be grated for a quicker dry. You can just spread things like peas or corn kernels out on the trays. Lay out all your slices without any overlapping and start up the machine. That's it.

Unlike fruit, most vegetables won't stick to your trays as they dry. Well, tomatoes might because they are so super juicy. But otherwise, you shouldn't need to worry about spraying trays or using the special inserts.

Blanching:

Even dry vegetables can start to deteriorate over time, because of the enzymes inside the plant tissues. In other words, you must deal with more than just outside mold and bacteria and dehydrating alone won't take care of it. A quick dip in boiling water is usually enough to kill off the enzymes, and then you're good to go.

Once you have your veggies all peeled, pitted and sliced, dunk them in boiling water for about 2 to 3 minutes. You don't want to actually cook them, but just scald them enough to stop the chemicals inside from working any more. Then take them out of the water and give them a good pat down to remove excess water.

If you really don't want to take the time to blanch, which can easily be the case when you have bushels of produce to dry, it isn't the end of the world. Your dried veggies will still last for months and be fully edible after you cook them up later.

How long to dry?

It's a little harder to generalize about drying vegetables because it's a really varied group of foods. Some are juicy, soft and full of water, and some are dense and tough by comparison. So expect a pretty wide range of time frames. Here are some of the more common veggies, and how long you should try them for. I've also added whether you need to do a blanch first.

- Carrots – 14 to 16 hours
- Green Beans – 10 to 12 hours

- Peas – 14 to 16 hours
- Zucchini – 6 to 8 hours
- Tomato – 14 to 16 hours
- Greens (like spinach or kale) – 8 to 10 hours
- Bell Peppers – 8 to 10 hours
- Broccoli – 10 to 14 hours
- Cauliflower – 12 to 14 hours
- Okra – 14 to 16 hours
- Pumpkin – 16 to 18 hours

Most of these will be either brittle or very leathery when they're done. Oh, and if you have a dehydrator with an adjustable thermostat, veggies dry best at 120F. If your machine is cooler than that, you may have to let them go longer.

Storing & Using Dried Vegetables:

So, to save your newly dried veggies for later, you just need to keep them in a dark container with a tightly fitting lid. Pretty much the same idea as any other dried food. They can last for several months, but generally not longer than a year.

Though you can eat some of these while dry, like crispy kale pieces or zucchini chips, you'll generally want to rehydrate your vegetables before you eat them. If you are adding them to a soup or stew, just toss in the dry pieces and simmer along with the dish until they have softened up. For other uses, add enough water to cover the dry bits and simmer until they rehydrate. Keep an eye on them though in case they need more water. Some vegetables will take a lot of moisture to get back to an edible state. Expect to let them cook for anywhere between 15 to 45 minutes. Some may take over an hour.

Dehydrated tomatoes (dried tomatoes)

The tomato is one of the most popular vegetables. They are easy to grow, cheap and healthy. Moreover, they can be used and processed in many different ways. They can be used in soups, sauces, salads and are delicious on bread. So now I will explain how to how to dry tomatoes. But first, how tomatoes are so important?

Vitamin A in tomatoes

Technically, the tomato is a fruit, but it is classified as a vegetable.

The main phytochemicals in tomatoes are carotenes, of which lycopene and beta-carotene dominate. Other lycopene includes lutein and zeaxanthin (these are not found in vegetables), which have been linked to many health benefits, including a lower risk of heart disease and cancer.

Lycopene is a powerful antioxidant.

Interestingly, according to the Linus Pauling Institute at Oregon State University, vitamin A activity cannot be derived from lutein, zeaxanthin, and lycopene.

In contrast, provitamin A carotenoids (α-carotene, β-carotene, and β-cryptoxanthin) can be converted by the body to retinol (vitamin A). Tomatoes provide the provitamin β-carotene, which can be converted to vitamin A.

According to the Linus Pauling Institute

Provitamin A carotenoids are less readily absorbed than preformed vitamin A, and the body must convert them to retinol and other retinoids. The efficiency of converting provitamin A carotenoids to retinol is highly variable depending on factors such as the matrix of food, food preparation. and digestion and absorbency. (source)

This is what the Weston Price Foundation has been saying for years: that vitamin A is best obtained by eating animal products that supply ready-made vitamin A, not provitamin carotenoids A.

It is important to note that the Linus Pauling Institute also states:

Carotenoids are better absorbed with fat during a meal. Cutting, mashing, and cooking vegetables that contain carotenoids in oil generally increases the bioavailability of the carotenoids they contain.

For intestinal carotenoids to be absorbed in the diet, they must be released from the food matrix and processed into mixed micelles (mixtures of bile salts and different types of lipids): food processing and cooking help to release carotenoids embedded in your food matrix and increase intestinal absorption. Also, the intake of carotenoids requires the presence of fats in a meal. Just 3 to 5 g of fat in a meal seems enough to ensure carotenoid absorption, although the minimum amount of dietary fat required for each carotenoid can vary. (source)

Once again, the Weston Price Foundation has insisted that provitamin A molecules do not readily convert to vitamin A, especially in children and others with potentially digestive disorders.

Also, you should eat fatty vegetables for better adsorption. This is based on the wisdom of the ages and science.

Nutrition in tomatoes

They are also a great source of vitamin C for immunity, potassium for heart health, folic acid for cell function, and vitamin K and blood clotting and bone health.

Tomatoes are a good source of fiber, providing about 1.5 grams per medium-sized tomato.

Other plant compounds in tomatoes include Naringenin, which is found in tomato peel. This flavonoid has been shown to reduce inflammation and protect against various diseases in mice.

How to dehydrate tomatoes?

Preparation time: according to the number of tomatoes.

Cooking time: 7 - 8 hours in the dehydrator.

Total time: 8 hours.

Instructions

Choose your fresh ripe tomatoes

With the help of mini plums, I quickly cut them in half

If you use large tomatoes, cut them into quarters and skip the stem

Add 1 gram of pure ascorbic acid (vitamin C) to a container of water.

Soak the tomatoes in this water for about 3-4 minutes.

This helps preserve color (this step is optional if you don't want to add anything)

Remove the tomatoes from the water and place them on the dehydrator trays.

Run the dehydrator at 135°F for 7-8 hours or 14 to 16 hours at 120 °F.

Tips: You can press down the tomatoes about halfway with a use of a spatula after about 2 to 2 1/2 hours to remove the juice. This will help them dry out faster. Just be careful, they can squirt at you!

Check them and run more if they are not dry enough.

Alternatively, you can dry them in the oven at 150° for 4-6 hours and If your tomatoes don't seem to be quite dry at the end, you can keep baking them. But another tip to get them even more dry is leaves them in the oven, with the oven turned off, and prop the door open with a wooden spoon. This will encourage air flow and they will dry even more. I used this technique a lot of times in the past for drying all kinds of foods and to make all kind of recipes when I didn't have a professional dehydrator.

Now a question will surely come to you…

How long do dried tomatoes last?

How long dried tomatoes last depends partly on how you store them. There are a couple options…

Refrigerate: You can keep them in an airtight container in the fridge for up to a week.

TIP: To preserve dried tomatoes for longer, you can store sun-dried tomatoes in olive oil. You can also throw in some Italian seasoning and even minced garlic if you like.

However, they still won't last as long as commercial dried tomatoes packed in oil, since the jar isn't sealed. That being said, the dried tomatoes will remain plump much longer this way. You'll still want to refrigerate the jar.

Freeze: If you want to make a huge batch of homemade dried tomatoes and preserve it for longer, the freezer is the way to go.

Freeze your dried tomatoes right on the baking sheet.

Once they are solid, you can transfer them to a freezer bag. If they are too rigid after thawing, you can reconstitute them in water or oil.

Broccoli

Broccoli is a good source of vitamin A, vitamin K, vitamin C, Folate, Choline, Potassium, Phosphorus, Calcium, Magnesium and has trace amounts of Niacin, Vitamin E, Thiamine.

Broccoli also contains Omega-3 and Omega-6 fatty acids.

Despite its nutritional value, broccoli does not have too many fans.

Many people have almost no steamed broccoli or broccoli that is overcooked and the color of old persimmon. Dried broccoli can be an attractive alternative. It offers the crisp, green color of raw broccoli, but has a slightly moderate flavor, making it a secret, healthy ingredient in many recipes. Plus dehydrating broccoli is easy whether you're using fresh or frozen! The only problem with frozen broccoli that I've noticed is that it tends to be very bitty.

Preparation time: 30 Minutes
Cooking Time: 12 Hours
Total time: 15 hours.

Ingredients:

- Fresh broccoli.

Instruction:

1. Wash the broccoli and pat dry. Cut into small florets and remove the stems. Cut the broccoli into 1/4-inch cubes.
2. Blanch in a small amount of boiling water for about 2 minutes.
3. Spread the broccoli pieces in a single uniform layer on one or more dehydration shelves making sure they don't touch each other.
4. Dry between 120F and 130F until it will be appearing very brittle.
5. Drying time for broccoli is between 9-14 hours
6. Transfer the broccoli to a clean work surface and cool to room temperature for about 2 hours.
7. Transfer to an airtight container and store.

Applications

Add chopped dried broccoli to the ricotta cheese filling in your favorite lasagna recipe. The broccoli softens as the lasagna cooks, and most of your guests will suspect it to be the usual parsley.

Make a green smoothie: Add 2 tablespoons of dried broccoli to your favorite smoothie recipe to add fiber and vitamins.

A great green smoothie recipe that I very like is:

1 cup of apple juice, 1/2 banana, 2 tablespoons of dried broccoli, 1/2 teaspoon of dried ginger, and 1/2 cup of ice.

Blend until completely smooth, about 3 minutes.

Cabbage

It's easy to have a lot of cabbage on hand. After all, a single cabbage seems to make gallons of coleslaw. When you come across leftover fresh cabbage, dehydration is a great preservation technique. Dried cabbage can quickly go into soups or chips. Cabbage it's rich in vitamins A, K and C, not to mention folate, potassium, calcium, phosphorus and certain trace minerals. A serving has only about 22 calories, while providing 2 grams of fiber and 1 gram of protein.

A world Cabbages:

There is a large variety of cabbage, this are the most common ones:

- Green – The one most familiar to Americans, especially if you like coleslaw, salads, stir fry or cabbage soup.

- Savoy – Considered the "prettiest" cabbage, it's often used in salads, especially with baby greens.

- White – Also known as a Dutch cabbage, it's very similar to the green cabbage in texture and density.

- Red – Great, thin sliced in salads or used in a red cabbage slaw.

- Napa (Chinese cabbage) – Used to make Korean Kimchi.

- Bok Choy – Looks a lot more like Swiss chard. A favorite in stir-fry. I like the leafy part in my salads.

- Brussels Sprouts – Looks like a "mini" green cabbage. I've called them hamster cabbages since I was a kid; my personal favorite, especially roasted!

Preparation time: 30 Minutes

Cooking Time: 12 Hours

Total time: 15 hours.

Ingredients:

- Fresh cabbage.

Instruction:

1. Wash the cabbage and remove the outer leaves from each head of cabbage that are too loose or wilted.

2. Clean and wash, then let stand or pat dry.

3. Cut the cabbage into quarters, and then into thin strips approximately 1/8" wide. Length can vary with no problem.

4. (Remember that there is no need to blanch the cabbage prior

to dehydrating)

5. Arrange the slices onto your dehydrator trays. They can nestle close together, even overlap just a touch

6. Turn on your dehydrator to the recommended temperature. Usually between 120F and 130F.

7. Dry between 8 – 11 hours depending on the thickness of the cabbage leaves. Don't forget to rotate your dehydrator trays for even drying.

8. After your cabbage pieces are fully dry, I suggest letting the cabbage stand at room temp for a night before packaging them for storage.

Storing:

There are a wide variety of choices as far as storage containers.

If it is long term storage, then I usually use everything from canning jars to mylar bags. In addiction I add an oxygen absorber in each container.

I don't suggest using plastic containers of any kind. I have had leakage problems no matter how carefully I store and stack them.

If the dehydrated cabbage is for more immediate consumption, such as on an outdoor adventure, then zip-loc bags will work just fine.

Applications;

Make spring rolls at home. Hydrate cabbage and drain, squeeze out excess water. Mix with minced cooked shrimp, chicken or pork, crushed garlic, powdered ginger, and water-diluted peanut butter. Roll in spring roll wrappers and fry in peanut oil.

Make quick pierogi (Polish dumplings) with dried cabbage. Hydrate the cabbage and drain it. Sauté in butter and add a pinch of salt and caraway seeds. Put a small teaspoon in a wonton wrap, fold in half and seal. Steam for 2-3 minutes and serve with sour cream.

Carrots

An effective way to prolong the shelf life of carrots is by dehydrating them.

Preparation time: 30 Minutes

Cooking Time: 16 Hours

Total time: 17 hours.

Ingredients:

- Fresh carrots

Instruction:

1. Remove the carrots' greens and ends. Using a vegetable brush, scrub the carrots until they're free from dirt.
2. Peel the carrots. You will end up with slightly bitter dehydrated carrots if you don't peel them.
3. Slice the carrots into ¼-inch circles. Thinner slices may fall through some dehydrator trays' ventilation holes. Thicker slices would take longer to dry.

4. Blanch the carrot slices using a steamer of boiling water for 2 minutes. This will retain the carrots' orange color. It'll also be quicker to rehydrate the carrots when they're blanched.

5. After 2 minutes of blanching, drop the slices into ice water immediately. You can also run cold water of the slices until they no longer feel warm.

6. Arrange the slices on the dehydrator trays. Make sure that no slices are touching each other.

7. Set the food dehydrator's temperature from 120F to 130F. Place the trays in the dehydrator and dry the carrots until they're completely dry. This may take up to 14-16 hours. (The dehydrating time will depend on the air's humidity and the thickness of the slices.)

8. Once the slices are crispy dry, turn off the food dehydrator and leave the carrots to cool at room temperature.

9. Transfer the carrots in storage containers.

10. The process of dehydrating with an oven is very similar to using a food dehydrator (See the steps for dehydrating using a food dehydrator). The only difference is the duration of the process.

11. Set the oven's temperature to 135°F or 125°F. If your oven doesn't go lower than 150°F, set the oven to the lowest temperature possible.

12. Roll up a dish towel and use it to prop the oven door open.

This will prevent the carrots from roasting.

13. This may take 6 to 8 hours, but it's best to constantly check on the carrots to make sure they're not roasted.

Storing:

Dehydrating carrots will already extend their shelf life. Storing them properly will make them last even longer.

After the dehydration process, let the carrots completely cool down before storing them.

Choose a high-quality airtight container for your carrots. You may also vacuum seal them in small batches. This will ensure that not all of your carrots will be wasted due to contamination.

Store the carrots in a dark and cool place. The ideal storage temperature would be 60F or less. Exposing dehydrated carrots to direct light and heat will shorten the shelf life of your carrots. It may also make the carrots lose their vitamin A content.

Tips:

Observe for water condensation inside freshly packaged dehydrated carrots. If you spot any water, it means that they need more time to dry. To avoid this, make sure that your carrots are completely free from moisture before storing.

Applications

Add dried carrot to your favorite green salad recipe to add a pop of color, sweetness, and nutrition. Dried carrot works well with cream and vinegar-based salad dressings.

Rinse the coleslaw by adding a little dried grated carrot to the fresh cabbage and dressing. The dressing will rehydrate the dried carrot.

Onions

Dehydrating onions is simple and one of the most practical things to dehydrate, especially if you grow your own. Of course, it makes sense to have them in your food storage too. Canning or freezing onions changes the texture and taste but dehydrating them then re-hydrating them when you're ready to cook is like having fresh onions. I can't tell that they have been dehydrated when I cook with re-hydrated onions.

Preparation time: 30 Minutes
Cooking Time: 16 Hours
Total time: 17 hours.
Ingredients:

- Some large yellow, white, or red onions

Instruction:

1. Remove the paper skins from the onions and discard them.
2. Wash and peel your onions.
3. Cut the onions into 1/4-inch slices.
4. Divide the onion into a single uniform layer on one or more dehydrator shelves.
5. Dry at 125 F for about 6-7 hours.
6. Place the onions on a clean work surface and allow it to cool to room temperature, about 2 hours.
7. Transfer to an airtight container and store.

Tips:

The first time I dehydrated onions I was worried because I washed all the trays, sprayed them with vinegar and even tried to air out the dehydrator for a bit. It still smelled like onions. I'm sure the smell would dissipate over time, but I use my dehydrator weekly if not daily. I discovered that if I just plan to dehydrate potatoes right after onions the smell is completely gone! It's like magic. I'm not worried at all if my potatoes pick up a hint of onions. I'd much rather have a hint of onion in my potatoes than my fruit.

Applications

Sprinkle dried onion slices over your favorite green bean casserole recipe to add the flavor and crispness of fried onions without extra calories or fat.

Prepare the onion powder by spraying it in a spice grinder or small food processor. Replace one by one with commercial onion powder. You can make red onion powder, which tastes like regular onion powder but is not sold in stores. Red onion adds a pop of color to any recipe.

Onion Flakes

Green onions or chives are brittle in the fresh state and do not stay in the refrigerator for long. Plus, recipes often call for just a few chives, leaving you with half a bunch of more spoiled in your product drawer. Drying chives is one way to extend the shelf life of these delicate vegetables. You can rehydrate them and use them as a substitute for fresh ones if you only need a small number of chives.

Ingredients

- 1 bunch of chives

- Wash the chives and pat dry. Trim and discard root tips and withered green tips. Cut the chives into 1/4-inch slices.

- Spread the tender onion slices in a single uniform layer on one or more dehydrator shelves. Dry at 125 ° F until the dehydrated onion falls in half when folded, about 2-3 hours.

- Transfer the chives to a clean work surface and cool to room temperature, about 2 hours. Transfer to an airtight container and store.

Dehydrate Corn

Dehydrated corn is one of the most addictive foods in the world. It's sweet, crisp, and easy to eat - you'll find that you want to eat it directly or by the handful. Dried corn is also a great addition to salads, sauces, and soups. It is an excellent way to bring the flavor of summer to every day of the year.

Preparation time: 40-60 minutes

Cooking time: 10 hours in the dehydrator.

Total time: 11 hours.

Ingredients:

- Fresh corn (if fresh corn isn't available, you can dehydrate frozen or canned corn as well)

Instruction:

Blanch corn by bringing bring a large pot of water to boil. Once boiling add cobs of corn to water, wait for water to return to boiling then boil for 4 minutes. Remove from heat and immediately cool in an ice water bath and drain well. Blanching ensures the aging enzymes in corn (the ones that turn corn from sweet to starchy) are destroyed and keeps your corn tasty sweet and delicious. (Do not add salt to water as this will toughen the corn.)

Cut corn off the cobs by placing cob end in the opening of a bundt pan. The pan will catch all the kernels and provide a steady base for the cob of corn as you run a sharp knife down the sides of the cob between the cob and the corn kernels.

Alternatively, cut a slice off the bottom of the corn cob to give you a level surface so you can hold the cob vertically on a cutting board without it wobbling. Run the knife down the sides of the cob.

Spread corn kernels on dehydrator trays in a single layer to allow for plenty of air circulation. Break any large pieces of corn apart into separate kernels for even drying.

Dehydrate at 125F (52C) until corn kernels are hard and dry. Depending on humidity levels this can take 8-12 hours.

Turn the dehydrator off and let them sit for another 60 minutes. This ensures that there won't be any condensation build up on the inside of the jars.

Now you can storing the fresh dry corn in airtight jars in a cool, dry, dark place for up to one year.

STRAWBERRIES

I love this whole process, from washing the juicy bright red fruits to cutting and seeing the vivid colors and seeing how, when you put them in your dehydrator, your whole house smells like a strawberry tart, and then everyone loves packing and enjoying the finished product.

Preparation time: 10/20 Minutes

Cooking Time: 6 Hours 10 Minutes

Total time: 7 hours.

Dried fruits are straightforward to make; strawberries are always a favorite! Cut into circles or triangles and enjoy the aroma of strawberry fields throughout your home as the sweet red fruit dries.

INSTRUCTIONS

1. Wash the fresh strawberries.

2. Cut the stems and cut them into 1/8 or ¼ inch rounds or

triangles.

3. Dry at 130-140° for 6-12 hours this prevent all the juices from leaking and creating a jelly film on the bottom.

4. Store for a few days in an airtight container at room temperature or in the freezer for long-term storage.

5. **TIPS:**

6. If you want to slice the strawberry, you can use a mushroom slicer instead of a knife to slice the fresh strawberries, however the strawberry slices will be a little thicker than if you cut them by hand, which may increase your baking time. Note that you want a veggie slicer with blades and not wires. Strawberries will cause the wires to bend, which creates unevenly sliced berries.

7. Obviously multiple baking sheets of strawberries can be baked at the same time. However, this will increase the amount of time needed for the strawberries to dry completely.

8. If you don't have a dehydrator, strawberries can be dried in a convection oven or using the convection setting of an oven. Depending on your oven, this may speed up the strawberry drying time. Be sure to check on the strawberries often after two hours to prevent burning!

DRY SNACK

Pumpkin Chips Baking Recipe

Pumpkin chips

Crispy and salty fries, without the clutter and cost of frying! It's the perfect alternative to potato chips and since I am a potato chip lover. They work best when cut into skinny slices with a very sharp knife. During the dehydration process, they curl up like conventional chips; it's fun!

Preparation time: 20-40 minutes
Cooking time: 18 hours in the dehydrator.
Total time: 19 hours.
Ingredients:

- A ripe and good-quality pumpkin

Instruction:

1. Before to start to dry your pumpkin make sure you scoop all the pumpkin pulp out of the pumpkin. I tried to use a knife in the beginning and realize that I was wasting pumpkin. I had a mess on my hand because of the shape of the pumpkin. I find that a spoon or ice cream scoop works the best.

2. After that you can cut the pumpkin and make sure you peel the tuff skin a way with a knife (a chef knife is the perfect choice). I would not use a peeler because it will become time consuming, and your fingers may have cuts and bruises once you're done with the peeler.

3. Now you can cut the pumpkin chips into a shape; any width will do because once they go in the dehydrator they will decrease in size. However, I would not cut them to thick they may take longer to become crispy. Oh, and don't use a mandolin I find it's just a waste of time but depending on the size of the pumpkin.

4. Set your dehydrator to 130F for an hour and turn it down to 120F for 16 hours or until there crunchy. The chips will not take longer than a day to be done.

Tips:

If you want to add some flavor to your pumpkin chips you can add 2 tbsps. of olive oil, 2 tsps. cayenne pepper, 1-2 tsp. salt, dash of garlic powder, and one too many dashes of black pepper. Make sure you coat the pumpkin very well with the spice mixture, also depending on how many trays of pumpkin chips you have. You may need to double the spice mixture if you're doing a big batch of pumpkin chips.

Sun Pumpkin Drying:

This is one of the natural methods of fruit and vegetable drying. An effective sun drying requires direct sunlight, outside temperature of 80°F – 90°F, and a humidity of less than 20%. Since the weather is uncontrollable, sun drying can be risky, for this reason I don't use this method very often.

After the same preparation of the pumpkin like we see before we can start to dry it with the power of the sun.

First place a clean cloth on a drying tray. Then, arrange the pumpkin slices on the tray. Make sure there is space between the slices, to allow air to circulate around (to speed up the drying process, cover the tray with a clear glass. This will also protect the slices from bugs and other insects.)

Bring the tray outside. Place it in an open space with direct sunlight. Make sure that the temperature outside is 80F – 90F or higher. During the night bring the tray inside, this will prevent the cool air to condense and add moisture back to the pumpkin slices.

Dry for 5-7 days. Flip the slices every five hours for uniform drying.

Check for dryness. The dried slices should be hard and brittle.

Beet Chips

Dried beets are sweet, crisp, and amazingly colorful. Beet drying maintains the soil of the vegetable and extends its shelf life.

Preparation time: 20 minutes

Cooking time: 4 hours in the dehydrator.

Total time: 5 hours.

Ingredients:

- 1/2-pound fresh beetroots

Instructions:

1. Slice the prepared beets paper-thin with a mandolin.
2. Lay the sliced beets out onto dehydrator trays.
3. Set the dehydrator to 125 F and dry the chips for approximately 3 to 4 hours. (Drying time could varies depending on the thickness of the chips and the humidity level near your dehydrator)
4. Serve or store in an airtight container. Depending on how

dried out the chips are, they are probably good for at least few weeks. They are easily squashed if stored in a bag, so opt for a sturdier container.

Applications

Add a handful of dried beets to your next red berry smoothie. The color of the beets will improve the color of your drink, and the sweetness of the beets will enhance the strawberry, cherry, or raspberry flavor.

Make a quick, cold beet soup. Mix the dried beets in a blender or food processor with plain yogurt or sour cream. Dilute with milk to the desired thickness and season with salt and pepper. Serve with extra dried beets and dried dill as a garnish.

Dried kale chips

Crispy kale fries are addictive but great for you. They're a much healthier option than potato chips. You can quickly and inexpensively make them at home with your food dryer. Raw food lovers can use a low-temperature method that produces a natural food product.

If you don't have a dehydrator, you can use the oven method to make kale fries faster or a warm oven to dry. Keep in mind that kale will shrink a bit during drying so you can keep the pieces more significant and do more than you think you need.

Preparation time: 10 minutes
Cooking time: 4 hours in the dehydrator.
Total time: 5 hours.
Ingredients

- 1 large bundle of kale (the variety)
- 2 to 3 teaspoons of extra virgin olive oil

- 3/4 teaspoon of salt

- Optional: 2 tablespoons nutritional yeast

- Optional: a pinch of cayenne pepper

Instructions

First you have to prepare the kale, remove the leaves from the petioles and the tough central rib. You don't want to dry the whole leaves because the central rod gets the consistency of the twigs, and they are not tasty. Compost the stems of the leaves or save them for the soup stock.

Wash the kale leaves and pat dry in a rotating salad or gently roll the leaves on a clean tea towel.

Tear the washed and dried leaves into pieces slightly larger than the chips; They shrink when dry.

Mix gently the kale in a large bowl with the extra virgin olive oil and salt. Massage the leaves thoroughly with your clean hands. All leaves should be covered more or less evenly with the oil.

If you like spicy flavors, add a little cayenne pepper.

You can also add nutritional yeast for a cheesy flavor.

Divide the sheets into several layers on the dehydrator trays. Please do not squeeze the leaves, or they will not dry evenly. It's okay if the sheets touch, but they shouldn't overlap.

Now it is time to dry it so set the dehydrator at 63° for 1 hour and after that reduce the heat to 46° and dry for an additional 3 to 4 hours until crispy dry.

Store:

You can also save it for later. To keep them crispy, it is important to let them cool completely. Once cooled, they can be stored in an airtight container at room temperature for 2-3 days.

You could also try adding a few grains of raw rice to the airtight container.

If your kale chips lose their crunch in storage, don't worry! You can re-crisp them in a low (93°) oven for 10 minutes, or in the dehydrator at 43° for an hour.

Beef Jerky

Jerky is one of the most effective ways to reserve left-over meat in good condition for a long time. Jerky simply is a result of a dehydrating process in which moisture and fat contained inside meat is got rid of, hence it is very good for your health. There are many types of jerky around the world, however, I think that beef jerky is the most popular and delicious.

Selecting a cut of meat:

Only choose a good quality lean cut with clear muscle grain, especially if you want to make tearing beef jerky. This kind of meat prevents your jerky from shredding after being torn. You can also slice the meat with the grain to make chewy beef jerky if you want.

Removing excess fat and slicing thin:

Excess fat enclosed will not only make the dehydrator process become longer but also your jerky spoils faster. All of them have to be removed. After cleaning carefully with water, you slice the meat into long pieces and each of them should not thicker than 0.7 cm. You can cut the meat with or against the grain, depend on what kind of jerky you want to make: the later slice style makes the jerky easier to chew. If you are a fresher in the kitchen and can't do like this, you can ask a butcher to do it for you with a small extra fee. Keeping your beef in the refrigerator for a while in order to make it easier for you to cut.

Marinating the pieces of meat:

You can use whatever recipe which is appropriate to your desire flavor of jerky. You can find them everywhere, from the internet to the recipe books. After marinating the pieces of meat, you have to wrap them tightly and put in the refrigerator for at least 8 hours for seasoning being absorbed deeply into the meat.

Cooking the meat:

Put your well-seasoned pieces of beef into a pot with a cover. Cook them in high temperature for about 2 minutes then flip them so that the outside of meat is cooked well-done. Next, you have to lower the temperature and cook continuously for about 20 minutes. If the meat seems to be dry, you can add 1 or 2 tablespoons of water. After that, you have to turn off the fire and let the meat get cold.

Thrashing the meat:

Using a pestle to thrash the pieces of meat, then make them become softer. If you want to make chewy beef jerky, you can skip this part.

Dehydrating the meat:

Now the important process is the state of starting your dehydrator to illustrate, this is a main role in the cooking process. And of course, the main objective in this part is to get rid of all the moisture from these slices of beef. Firstly, you have to arrange all the beef pieces into trays. Remember to leave enough room between each piece of meat because the air which contains evaporated moisture need space for air circulation process. As you know, the faster air current, the faster the food reaches to dehydrating state. Then, you turn on the food dehydrator, set the temperature to maximum, normally around 155F degrees. Because the humidify level of beef jerky and the thickness of each slice vary, depend on what recipe you follow. Hence, there is no particular time setting for the dehydrating process. However, in this case, you can set the appropriate time for about 6 hours. And you have to remember to check the humidity of the beef jerky frequently after 2 hours, and every 30 minutes from then on until the jerky satisfies your requirement. After the process is done, you should also cut through some pieces of beef jerky to make sure that there is no raw meet inside. Although meat is cooked before, but carrying a careful check is necessary to prevent any harm for your health. At last, the finished product should have a deep brown or burgundy color.

Dehydrator is a convenient device to dry food. It makes this process become easier and more interesting. By following all these steps mentioned above, I hope that all of you can make your desired home-made beef jerky. Good luck!

How to conserve beef jerky:

One of the top questions is "how long does jerky stay good?"

The simple answer is 1-2 months for homemade jerky and 1 year for commercial jerky. Now with that said, don't go leaving an open bag of jerky sitting in the sun and expect it to last 2 months.

The reason jerky even came about was to solve a problem of keeping a protein source edible for long periods of time when food was not available. Dehydrating meat removes moisture so that bacterial or fungal enzymes cannot react with the meat which in turn preserves it from spoiling. What started as a Native American process of preserving meat for necessity has evolved into great tasting snack food.

Remember that fat is the enemy when it comes to making jerky. Fat will spoil fast and make the jerky go rancid quicker than it would if there wasn't fat. Purchase lean meat and trim all visible fat before drying.

Now let's see the various conservation methods…

Storage (lack of oxygen):

This is one of the simple methods I know of storing food and it is the one of the main reasons that commercial beef jerky stays good for so long is because they make sure there is no oxygen in their finished product packaging. This is normally done by shooting nitrogen into their packages to flush out the oxygen before inserting the jerky and sealing. I don't know about you, but I don't have nitrogen laying around the house for jerky making! So here are the best practices you can do when storing your jerky to keep it fresh longer.

Before start to explain the different process to subtract oxygen to store the beef jerky, I have some advice to give you: If you feel that your jerky is a bit too moist you can store it in a paper bag for a short (for a day or two) in a paper bag will create a wick affect that allows the jerky to expel any existing moisture which will help it last longer. This can be done transferring it to a jar or zip lock.

1) Zip lock and paper bags

If you are looking to store your jerky short term, then storing in a simple zip lock bag is suffice. This should keep it good for at least 3-4 weeks or more.

Tip: If you feel that your jerky is a bit too moist, you can always add a small food grade desiccant bag to it. You will know if it's going bad because it will generally become much drier and will usually turn a darker color. The smell of it will often slightly change as well.

2) Dry canning

Dry canning your beef jerky in mason jars is a great way to preserve it for months.

Here's how to dry can your jerky:

- Set your oven to 350 F
- Remove the lids from your mason jars and set them on a cookie sheet.

- Put the jars in the oven for around 10 minutes.
- Remove the jars from the oven using mitts and then quickly set your jerky strips inside of them.
- Screw on the lids of the jars and let them cool to room temperature. As the jars cool, they will create a vacuum seal. You will know when they are beginning to create a vacuum because you will hear a popping sound coming from them.

3) Vacuum Seal Bags

Using Vacuum seal bags to store your jerky is the best way to store your jerky long term. They allow you to keep the moisture in and the air out which is great because your jerky will still be somewhat soft but will have no oxygen to spoil and also it preserves the flavor and texture of your jerky.

Cure:

Most commercial producers use a cure consisting of sodium nitrite to extend the life of their jerky to 1 year. This prevents bacteria that could survive in meat that is only dried and not cooked. It is not a requirement to use a cure and most homemade recipes do not include one. Therefore you will heat homemade jerky to 155-160° F, allowing your jerky to stay bacteria free without a cure.

One last tip:

If wanting to keep jerky for longer than 1-2 months, you can freeze it for up to 6 months. If in addiction to that you vacuum sealed bags or jars, they will stay good for even longer we're talking of 12 months.

But freezing can alter the taste of jerky and I personally don't recommend it. A better practice is to make smaller batches and eat within a month or two, rather than making a big batch and having too much jerky at once.

Alternatively...The Oven:

Probably the main question I hear from friends is how to make beef jerky without a dehydrator. It's totally possible in the oven. But in order for it to cook evenly, I recommend laying the jerky out on wire racks that are placed on top of foil-covered baking sheets. I know that some people like to just lay the jerky out directly on the oven racks themselves, and then place a sheet of aluminum foil on the bottom of the oven to catch the dripping juices, but I've tried it and — heads up — it's messy. So instead, I recommend the wire rack method.

Remember that even with the oven set at its lowest heat, it is still hotter than a food dehydrator. I believe this dries the beef faster and locks in the flavor.

The key to any delicious jerky is first letting the beef sit in a flavorful marinade for several hours, like mentioned before.

When you are ready to cook, preheat the oven to 175°F. Adjust the racks to the upper-middle and lower-middle positions. Line two large baking sheets with aluminum foil, and place wire cooling racks on top of each sheet. Lay the strips out in a single layer on the wire racks. Bake until the beef jerky until it is dry and firm, yet still a little bit pliable, about 4 hours, flipping the beef jerky once about halfway through. (Cooking times will vary based on the thickness of your meat.) Remove jerky and enjoy it.

Canadian-style ham and bacon

Choose a lean Canadian-style ham or bacon ready to eat. Cut all the fat. Since they are prepared products, Canadian-style ham and bacon can be dried without further cooking. However, the pork will be more tender if it is rehydrated if it is heated before drying; fry it as if you were serving hot meat. Cut Canadian-style ham and bacon 3/16-inch thick or slightly thinner, then cut into ¼ to ½-inch strips of no more than 2 inches.

Dried meat will be oily on the surface. Pat them with paper towels while they are still hot to remove the oil spheres on the surface and place a new paper towel in the storage container with the dried meat.

Drying Methods: Canadian Style Ham and Bacon
DEHYDRATOR / CONVECTION OVEN

Use screens on trays or racks.

Pieces of Canadian ham and bacon generally take

5 to 10 hours at 145 ° F.

OVEN (NO CONVECTION)

Use screens in racks. Stir the pieces several times during drying. At 145 ° F, Canadian-style slices of ham or bacon can dry for just 5 hours or 15 hours.

Cooking test: rigid, with a deep pink color; the center should look completely dry when cutting apart.

YIELD: 1 pound Canadian-style ham or bacon provides approximately ¾ cup dry chunks. When rehydrated, 1 cup of baked ham or Canadian-style pieces of bacon makes about 1¼ cups.

TO USE: To rehydrate, combine in a skillet with water to coat generously. Cover and simmer for about 1 hour, or until meat is tender. Drain and use on any cooked dish that requires Canadian-style cooked bacon or ham. Rehydrated meat has a firm texture.

Grated fruit and vegetable salad

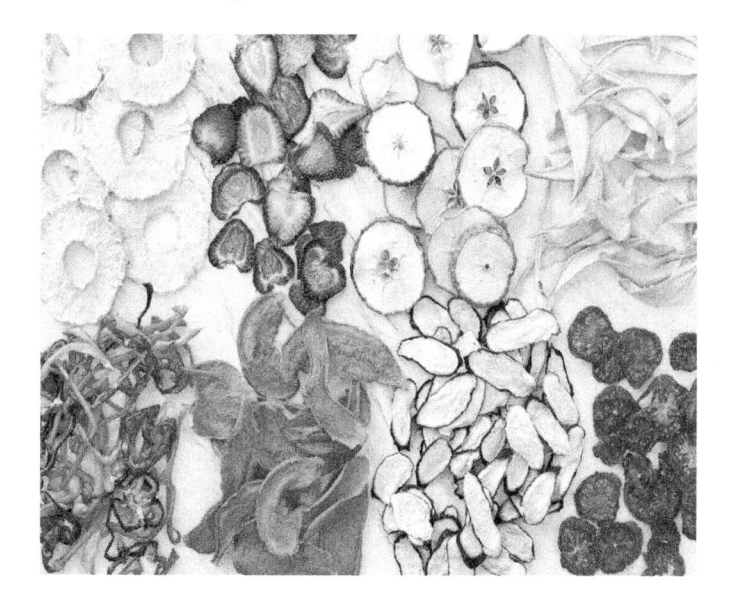

This delicious fruit salad combines the sweetness of the fruit with the crispness and nutrition of the vegetables.

Makes 8 servings

- ½ cup dried grated carrots
- ½ cup dried pineapple cubes
- ½ cup dehydrated grated apples
- ½ cup dried grated zucchini
- ½ cup of dried grapes
- ¼ cup dry grated coconut
- 4 cups boiling water
- 2 cups of whipped cream

- 2 tablespoons icing sugar
- 2 teaspoons of vanilla extract

1. In a large heat-resistant bowl, combine the dehydrated ingredients, pour boiling water, cover and let stand 15 minutes to rehydrate.

2. In a medium bowl, beat the cream, icing sugar, and vanilla together with an electric mixer until smooth peaks form. Put aside.

3. Drain the rehydrated ingredients into a strainer. Dry the bowl and replace the rehydrated items. Mix the whipped cream and place it in an airtight container. Refrigerate for 6 hours and serve.

DESSERTS

We all love dessert! What is eaten for dinner is not complete if not followed by a little sweetness. This chapter will help you prepare delicious and healthy desserts that your whole family will love. By adding dried fruit, you can take your desserts to the next level. Plus, we'll show you how to introduce a little extra nutrition by adding vegetables that naturally sweeten your cakes and muffins.

Lavashak

Lavashak, or Persian style fruit leather, is an easy to make snack of dried fruit dried out in your oven! Healthy, tasty and vegan! These delicious snacks are originally made in Iran for the first time. It was the consequence of finding out about the abundance of summer fruits, ancient Iranians decided to dry a plenty of them for severe winters.

Fruit Roll-Ups are made of fruits like Plum, sour cherries, Zereshk, Apricot, kiwi which all have mostly sour-based taste.

Here I will explain how to make your Persian style fruit leather with the most traditional fruit, the plums. However you can replace the plums with any fleshy fruit (apple, peach, cherry etc.) you want!

Now let's move on to the practical part…

HOW TO MAKE LAVASHAK

Preparation time: 40 Minutes

Cooking Time: 4-6 Hours

Total time: 7 hours.

Ingredients:

- 6 medium plums
- ½ cup water
- Dash of salt
- Spices such as cinnamon and nutmeg (optional)

Instructions:

1. Wash and roughly chop the plums.
2. Place the plums, water and salt into a sauce pot and bring to a simmer over medium heat.

3. Let simmer for 30 minutes, stirring occasionally, until the fruit is mushy to the point of falling apart. (Watch the water level carefully and add a bit more over time if it starts to burn)
4. Using an immersion blender (or transfer the contents to a blender), blend the fruit well.
5. Continue to blend until no chunks are visible and the consistency is very smooth.
6. Preheat your oven to 200 F.
7. Line a cookie sheet with parchment paper.
8. Spread the fruit mixture on the cookie sheet (here's where the cake spatula comes in handy) in an even layer about ¼ inch thick.
9. Bake in the oven for about 4-5 hours, checking every hour.
10. The lavashak is done when there is no visible wetness, it is no longer sticky, it has a smooth surface and the fruit leather separates easily from the paper.
11. Cut into strips and enjoy!
12. Alternatives to the oven you already know that you can use food dehydrator. I suggest to put the tray in the weber grill, and leaving covered, in the sun all day. This is good trick.
13. Obviously, it can be done as the Persians did in antiquity, just try to tent the tray with some cheesecloth and leave it outside in the sun on a hot day.

Store:

To store it, roll it in plastic wrap, put it in an airtight container and store in the refrigerator or freezer.

Tips:

You can keep the peels on the plums, it adds wonderful flavor and color!

Very spicy gingerbread cookies

I just developed this recipe to use with dried ginger. If you make these cookies with store-bought ground ginger, they will be too strong. If you like gingerbread cookies, give it a try - dehydrated ginger has its unique flavor, which I think is much better than store-bought.

This is the ingredients to make 24 cookies:

- 2¼ cups all-purpose flour
- 2 teaspoons of baking soda
- 1 teaspoon ground cinnamon
- ¾ cup (1½ sticks) butter, softened
- 1¼ cups more ⅓ cup sugar
- ½ cup of molasses
- 1 large egg
- 1 tablespoon coarse ground dry ginger

1. Preheat oven to 350 ° F. Sprays a large baking sheet with cooking spray.

2. In a medium bowl, combine flour, baking powder, and cinnamon.

In a large bowl, beat butter and 1¼ cups sugar until creamy. Add the molasses, egg, and ginger and beat until smooth. Add flour mixture in three additions, mixing well after each.

4. Roll the dough into 1-inch balls and roll the remaining ⅓ cup of sugar to coat. Place 2 inches apart on the baking sheet. Press them with the palm of your hand to make a thick disc. Bake until edges are lightly browned, 10 to 12 minutes. Chill on the baking sheet for 5 minutes, then remove to a wire rack to cool completely. Store in an airtight container.

Raw Crackers

Carrot juice is so good for you, but it generates massive amounts of pulp. And, to be totally honest, I often throw it out. To relieve the guilt, I often save it, even freeze it. But eventually, most of it ends up in a compost pile or down the disposal.

But wait a minute… I can create a recipe to reuse this "refuse".

So I decided to make raw crackers

This healthy, plant-based Gluten-Free Vegan Raw Carrot Pulp and Flax Seed Crackers dehydrator recipe is the perfect solution to use leftover carrot juice pulp in an easy snack made with only 7 clean, real food ingredients and they're vegan, gluten-free, dairy-free, egg-free, nut-free, oil-free, paleo-friendly.

Preparation time: 20 Minutes

Cooking Time: 15 Hours

Total time: 16 hours.

Ingredients:

For the crackers:

- 3 cups organic carrot pulp
- 3/4 cup filtered/purified water
- 1/2 cup organic ground flax seeds
- 1 organic tomato
- 1 tablespoon organic lemon juice
- For the add-ins:
- 1/2 cup organic chia seeds
- 1/2 cup organic sesame seeds

Instructions:

1. Please Note: This recipe requires 10-12 dehydrating time.
2. Add all the ingredients for the crackers in a blender and blend until everything is well combined and the mixture has a thick paste-type consistency.
3. After you've made the cracker mixture, transfer the cracker mixture to a medium-size bowl and add the chia seed + sesame seed add-ins, then stir them into the cracker mixture.
4. Spread the cracker mixture evenly onto the non-stick dehydrator sheets of a dehydrator tray, taking care to not spread it too thick or too thin.
5. Dehydrate at 105 F for approximately 8-12 hours (I suggest

doing this overnight)

6. Remove the crackers from the sheet and transfer them to a mesh dehydrator tray and dehydrate for an additional 2-6 hours, or until they are hard and crisp.

7. Cut into small bite-size cracker pieces and store in an air-tight container.

Store:

Now we already know that the dehydrator will remove all the moisture from the crackers so it's very important that you properly store the crackers to keep them crisp. Make sure you store them in an air-tight container until ready to serve. Even the air has moisture in it so leaving them out in the open will cause them to get soft. I advise to use glass storage containers for dehydrated items, as well as for other food storage.

Chocolate and Banana Fruit Roll

Preparation time: 5 Minutes

Cooking Time: 10Hours

Total time: 10 hours.

Ingredients:

- 4 bananas
- 2 tablespoons cocoa powder
- 1 tablespoon brown sugar

Instructions:

1. Wash the bananas.
2. Add bananas, sugar, and cocoa into blender and puree till smooth.
3. Line a food dehydrator rack with parchment paper or use the fruit leather screen and pour the mixture into the tray 1/4 inch thick.
4. Dry at 130 degrees Fahrenheit for up to 10 hours. You may want to flip the leather halfway through, dry until no moist spots are left and it separates easily from the paper.

Peanut Butter Banana Chips

Peanut Butter Banana Chips are so easy to prepare you won't mind if your kids help. The instructions are a breeze and you can forget about them in your dehydrator overnight. These chips are great to include with school lunches or toss them in a diaper bag when you're on the go.

Okay I know it isn't a healthy recipe but, HEY,

sometimes we must put our minds aside and do some sin of gluttony. You Only Live Once.

Preparation time: 10 Minutes

Cooking Time: 8 Hours

Total time: 9 hours.

Ingredients:

- 5 bananas
- ¼ cup creamy peanut butter

Instructions:

1. Slice the bananas into coins about ¼ inch thick.
2. Combine the bananas and peanut butter in a container with a lid.
3. Place the lid on the container and give it a good shake until the banana slices are coated with the peanut butter. If the peanut butter is too thick and not mixing well, add 2 to 3 tablespoons of water.
4. Remove the individual slices of banana from the container and place them on the dehydrator trays. Leave space between so they are not touching.
5. Dehydrate at 160° for 8 hours.
6. Remove from the dehydrator and refrigerate in an airtight container.

CONCLUSION

In this guide, we have seen how storing our food is as essential as consuming them. The essence of storing food is for them to be consumed later. If all we do is eat and waste the remains, then there would soon be nothing left for humanity's consumption.

Among all the food storing methods, storing through by dehydrating has been our cardinal point.

A food dehydrator is a device that removes moisture from food to aid in its preservation. A food dehydrator uses a heat source and air flow to reduce the water content of foods. The water content of food is usually very high, typically 80% to 95% for various fruits and vegetables and 50% to 75% for various meats. Removing moisture from food restrains various bacteria from growing and spoiling food. Further, removing moisture from food reduces the weight of the food. Thus, food dehydrators are used to preserve and extend the shelf life of various foods. In addition removing water causes the flavors of the food to become more concentrated. Many culinary techniques make use of food dehydrators.

Bacteria and fungi (yeasts and molds) are the principal types of microorganisms that cause food spoilage and food-borne illnesses. Foods may be contaminated by microorganisms at any time during harvest, storage, processing, distribution, handling, or preparation. The primary sources of microbial contamination are soil, air, animal feed, animal hides and intestines, plant surfaces, sewage, and food processing machinery or utensils.

Bacteria are unicellular organisms that have a simple internal structure compared with the cells of other organisms. The increase in the number of bacteria in a population is commonly referred to as bacterial growth by microbiologists. This growth is the result of the division of one bacterial cell into two identical bacterial cells, a process called binary fission. Under optimal growth conditions, a bacterial cell may divide approximately every 20 minutes. Thus, a single cell can produce almost 70 billion cells in 12 hours. The factors that influence the growth of bacteria include nutrient availability, moisture, pH, oxygen levels, and the presence or absence of inhibiting substances (e.g., antibiotics). The oxygen requirements for optimal growth vary considerably for different bacteria. Some bacteria require the presence of free oxygen for growth and are called obligate aerobes, whereas other bacteria are poisoned by the presence of oxygen and are called obligate anaerobes. Facultative anaerobes are bacteria that can grow in both the presence and absence of oxygen. The oxygen reduction potential is a relative measure of the oxidizing or reducing capacity of the growth medium.

Bacteria also require a certain amount of available water for their growth. The availability of water is expressed as water activity and is defined by the ratio of the vapor pressure of water in the food to the vapor pressure of pure water at a specific temperature. Therefore, the water activity of any food product is always a value between 0 and 1, with 0 representing an absence of water and 1 representing pure water. Most bacteria do not grow in foods with a water activity below 0.91; although some bacteria (those able to tolerate high salt concentrations) can grow in foods with a water activity lower than 0.75. Growth may be controlled by lowering the water activity—either by adding solutes such as sugar, glycerol, and salt or by removing water through dehydration.

Also, most foods are dehydrated at temperatures of 130 °F, or 54 °C, although meats being made into jerky should be dehydrated at a higher temperature of 155 °F, or 68 °C, or preheated to those temperature levels, to guard against pathogens that may be in the meat. The key to successful food dehydration is the application of a constant temperature and adequate air flow. Too high a temperature can cause food to be hardened. This refers to food that is hard and dry on the outside but moist on the inside, and therefore vulnerable to spoiling on the inside.

The major key in optimal dehydration is to remove moisture as quickly as possible at a temperature that does not seriously affect the flavor, texture and color of the food. If the temperature is too low in the beginning, bacteria may survive and grow before the food is adequately dried. If the temperature is too high and the humidity too low then the food may harden on the surface. This makes it more difficult for moisture to escape and the food does not dry properly. A trial-and-error approach often is needed to decide which techniques work best for the dehydrator and food type you are using.

This book has provided a sufficient guide on the advantages of dehydration, disadvantages and the importance.

We have also critically examined other methods of preserving foods. The advantages of these methods too were meticulously discussed along with their disadvantages.

In the subsequent chapter, we discussed the degrees of heat needed for dehydrating several foods, fruits and vegetables. Herbs also have their dehydrating temperature.

Before spilling the beans on the importance of exercises, we talked about the various challenges people encounter when dehydrating food. You surely don't want to create a bigger mess from a simple common error. Most time, the problems we face while dehydrating our fruits, herbs or food can easily be corrected just by going through the right guide.

All through the pages of this guide, I emphasize the importance of reading the manual that comes with the equipment.

Of great importance is the deliberate faithfulness to balanced diets. Under general healthy tips, I discussed the importance of religiously sticking to balanced diets. You surely don't want to exhibit the negative consequences of not eating a balanced diet.

Most of the sickness and illness can be prevented by sticking to healthy eating. Medical conditions like obesity, high blood pressures and etc. can be corrected with balanced diets.

Another crucial matter discussed under the healthy tips is the matter of exercises. Balanced diets and exercises go hand in hand for anyone who is willing to live a perfect life.

It is usually strenuous to exercise when it becomes recommended to fight a medical condition. Why not make it a daily activity?

In the modern world, the comfort of remote controls for virtually everything has added to our stilled activities. Most people are can now be seated in a spot for longer hours. Consequently, the body fats increase and blocks the free flow of air in and out of the lungs.

The recent addiction to social media pages too is one huge factor responsible for many unhealthy issues. Exercising the body regularly is a greatly rewarding activity.

Under food dehydration, I explained the differences between food dehydration and drying. The concepts are often used interchangeably but they mean different things.

While every dehydration process requires some level of drying, dried foods may not necessarily be dehydrated. Dehydration has to do with deliberately applying heat to food to reduce the water content.

Early men dehydrated their foods through sun drying. Dehydration is therefore the oldest method of food preservation.

You may want to ask though; why do we dehydrate food?

Although the importance of dehydration has been extensively treated in this guide, as a recap, I'd quickly bullet some reasons as to why you should consider getting a dehydrator in your home.

- Dehydrating food would not lead to nutrient loss.
- Dehydrating food does reduce the size of the food and makes it easy to pack.
- Foods dehydrated can last over a long period of time.
- Dehydrated foods can be converted into forms that can endure the rigor of transportation and time before getting to their final destination.
- Are there any disadvantages? Well, any idea that has advantages must have corresponding disadvantages. Although, we have treated the disadvantages in this guide, I shall take this concluding paragraph to bullet some of the disadvantages here.
- When you dehydrate your food, the appearance may change. Usually the familiar taste of a changed food is always disagreeable. Most people want to eat what looks like what they already know.
- Dehydrating food requires a level of knowledge. An error in the process can discourage the user from subsequent attempts.
- Dehydration may change the flavors and taste of the food, fruits or vegies. While many people, like me, would argue that it advances the tastes of food, some would disagree.

Despite the few disadvantages, the benefits of dehydration, far outweighs the disadvantages. Considering all connected topics, one can safely conclude that dehydration is indeed one of the best methods of preserving foods.

Printed in Great Britain
by Amazon